STAINED GLASS
PATCHWORK
for Christmas

Gail Lawther

SUPPLIERS

Ordinary bias binding is available from most sewing shops and haberdashery departments. Fusible bias binding, and the tools for making your own, are available from many specialist quilt suppliers; for your nearest stockist, contact Winbourne Fabrics Ltd, Unit 3A, Forge Way, Brown Lees Road Industrial Estate, Kuypersley, Stoke-on-Trent. ST8 7DN (tel 01782 513380).

If you enjoy this foray into stained glass patchwork, and would like to know more about Gail's books, patterns, talks, videos and workshops on the subject, contact her at the Teamwork address below, or via her website: www.gail-quilts-plus.co.uk.

First published in 2002 by
Traplet Publications Limited
Traplet House, Severn Drive, Upton upon Severn,
Worcestershire WR8 0JL

Publisher: Tony Stephenson

Text © Gail Lawther

All photographs © Christopher Lawther, unless otherwise stated
All illustrations by Gail Lawther, © Traplet Publications
Studio scans and pre-press work by Neil Blowers

ISBN 1 900371 80 4
British Library Cataloguing in Publication Data
A catalogue record for this book is available from the British Library

Designed and edited by Teamwork, Christopher and Gail Lawther,
44 Rectory Walk, Sompting, Lancing, West Sussex BN15 0DU
Set in Galliard and Stone Sans

Printed by Stephens & George
Goat Mill Road, Dowlais, Merthyr Tydfil CF48 3TD

STAINED GLASS PATCHWORK for Christmas

Gail Lawther

TRAPLET
PUBLICATIONS

Contents

Introduction

I've always loved stained glass; the strong lines and bright colours appeal to my sense of design, and I'm constantly amazed at the variety of styles and approaches that people who design stained glass build into their creations. Of course the craft of stained glass began in churches; it was a great way of combining the tasks of letting in light, decorating the surroundings, and telling basic bible stories. Although this began in mediaeval times, one of the things that I love about church stained glass is that it's grown and developed through the centuries; some of the modern stained glass is breathtaking in its beauty and creativity.

Well, what does all this have to do with patchwork and quilting? If you're reading this book, you probably already know the answer to that question: the technique known as stained glass patchwork. I came across this technique quite early on in my quilting career, and because of my interest in ordinary stained glass, it caught my attention straight away with its bold lines and stylised designs. I then discovered that it was a very quick way of putting together even quite large quilts, because there's no seaming or piecing involved; although it's called stained glass **patchwork**, it's really a method of appliqué. And it seems to lend itself particularly well to Christmas designs – as you'll see in the projects in this book.

Stained glass patchwork is an exceptionally easy technique, too, which makes it perfect for beginners, and it's also a very forgiving technique; you can make quite large mistakes and still get away with them! I quickly decided that stained glass patchwork had my name written all over it; although I work in many different techniques, this one is still my favourite, and it's the one I return to again and again.

If you're completely new to stained glass patchwork, have a careful read of the sections where I explain the basic technique; you'll soon see just how easy and straightforward it is. Work with ordinary cotton fabrics, and begin with one of the really easy projects, such as the hearts on page 19, one of the 'baby makes' on page 46, or the crazy Christmas star on page 26. Once you've built up your confidence, try something slightly larger such as the window scene on page 41, or the embellished tree on page 22. You'll find that I've given each project an easiness rating, with details of any points to watch out for; this will help you to choose the right project for your 'comfort zone'! For many of the small and medium projects, I've also included a sequence of step-by-step diagrams; these show you exactly in which order to add the lines of bias binding, which takes any guesswork out of the stitching.

PHOTOS: MAL LUFF

If you're already a confident stitcher, you'll probably already know just how easy the technique of stained glass patchwork is. You may well be able to go straight to the more complex projects, and you might like to experiment with more challenging fabrics, such as silks, metallics and satins – I've included some pointers on using these on pages 7-8. For the more complex projects I haven't included step-by-step stitching sequences, as by this stage you'll be used to the idea of working out the T-junctions (see page 2)!

These examples of old and new stained glass are both in St Nicolas Church, Old Shoreham; the modern window was designed by Sue Wallis

Whatever your experience as a stitcher, you'll find projects to suit your abilities, and a wide range of styles, from the folk-art reindeer on page 39, through the traditional crib triptych on page 36, to the more modern blue and gold star on page 28. Many of the projects also make excellent Christmas presents; try the Bethlehem scene on page 34, the poinsettia on page 16, or the star on page 26 – and you'll find that you can stitch a whole series of Christmas heart decorations (page 19) very quickly and easily. I hope that you'll enjoy trying out the different projects, and that stitching them – and using them when they're finished – will enhance your enjoyment of the whole festive season.

THE BASIC TECHNIQUE

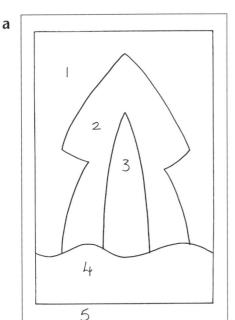

a

Building up the design

Let's look first at how the basic technique of stained glass patchwork works. You'll see from this sequence just how easy it is; any of the variations that I use in the projects within the book are all just developments of this same basic technique.

1 Start by drawing your design out full-size on plain paper; when you're happy with the design, go over the lines with black felt pen so that they're good and strong. Put numbers on the different parts of the design; this will help you when you're putting all the patches back together again later (**a**).

2 Now you need to pick a foundation fabric to build your design on – this should be something like loosely-woven cotton, sheeting, firm muslin. All of this foundation fabric is going to be covered, so don't bother to use anything smart! Use a light colour – white or cream, ideally – so that you can see the line of your design through it. (If your finished design will have a light-coloured background, such as the partridge in a pear tree on page 16, you can use the background fabric as your foundation fabric.)

b

3 Cut a piece of foundation fabric the same size as your design and lay it over your drawing; put a couple of pins in so that the drawing doesn't slip, then trace all the lines of the design in soft pencil (**b**). All of these lines are going to be covered, so you don't need to worry about removing them later. It can be useful to write the numbers in on your foundation fabric too, but if you do this use a pale crayon, otherwise the numbers may show through any light-coloured fabric patches.

4 Now you need to cut up your original drawing, so if you think you might want to do the same design again, take a photocopy or trace a copy before you cut. Cut along all the marked lines to create templates for cutting your fabric patches (**c**).

5 The next thing to do is to decide which fabric you're going to be using for which part of the design. If you're not sure straight away, cut a little snippet from each fabric and move them around your design until you're happy with the combination.

6 When you've chosen the fabric for each patch, lay each template **right side up** on **the right side** of the fabric and pin it in position, then cut around the edges – or, if you find it easier, you can draw round the template with a pencil and then cut. Remember that, as you're not joining the patches, you don't need to worry about the grain of the fabric and you don't need to add any seam allowances – but if you want to add a little extra safety margin, you could cut just a fraction outside the edges of the template, say 1mm.

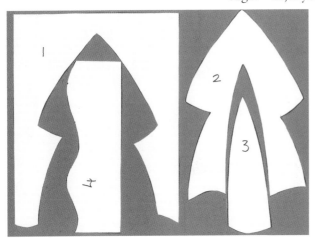

c

7 When you've cut all the patches out, lay them right side up in their correct positions on the foundation fabric, just like assembling a jigsaw. Once they're all in the right places, pin them in position (**d**). (You can tack them in position if you prefer, but for a design of this size it isn't usually necessary.)

8 You've now assembled your basic design, and it's time to start adding the bias binding! The only thing you need to remember when you're building up a stained glass patchwork design is to begin with the T-junctions. These are the lines tha form a T with a longer line, just like when you're driving and you come to a T-junction - you can either go right or left, but you can't go straight ahead. In this design the first T-junctions are on the the line which forms the inside tree shape. The reason you begin with a T-junction is because, as you lay binding down on this line, you're going to end up with a raw end of binding where the line stops; if you stitch this line of binding into position first, you'll cover the raw end with the snowline – and so on, through the design.

And, even if you get it wrong occasionally, and come to a line and realise that you should have stitched it earlier, the worst that can happen is that you just slit a few stitches and tuck the raw end underneath!)

9 Lay the binding along the line between the two patches, straddling the two fabrics evenly to cover the raw edges (**e**), and pulling the binding into nice smooth curves – don't flatten the curves out, but keep them flowing and strong. Pin each first section of binding in place; if you pin across the binding, you anchor the fabric each side as well as the binding, and you can stitch carefully over the pins if you're machine-stitching without them keeping on catching in your machine foot. Again, you can tack the binding in place if you prefer, but it's often not necessary for small designs, and tacking just adds work.

10 Once the first lines are pinned in position, you need to stitch down each edge of the bias binding. You can do this by hand or by machine – I'll talk about each method in detail in a minute; for the moment, I've stitched this design using a small zigzag stitch in a matching thread. Once you've stitched all the lines in position, remove the pins and trim the ends of the bias if necessary.

11 Carry on building up the design and covering the raw ends in exactly the same way; you can see in **f**, **g** and **h** how I've added the different lines in sequence. If you're stitching a simple curve like the inner outline of the tree, where each part only curves in one direction, stitch the inside of the curve first; if you do it the other way round, you can sometimes find that the inside edge is stretched too strongly and puckers a little.

12 Of course there are various ways in which you can finish off a stained glass patchwork design; with a panel like this, an easy way is to back it and bind the edges with one piece of fabric. Cut a piece of black fabric about an inch larger all round, then fold the edges of this backing over the front to create a binding all the way around. Another way, which creates a larger design, is to cut a frame from a contrasting fabric; you can put this round the edge of the design, and then add binding where the fabrics meet in just the same way as before; you could finish off the final design with an outside black binding as for the smaller design, or you could turn the raw edges of the frame to the back and hem them.

And that's all there is to the basic technique – it really is that easy!

d

e

f

g

h

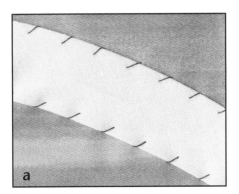

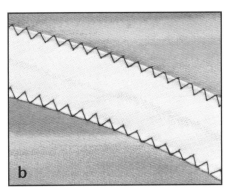

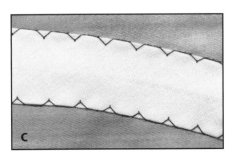

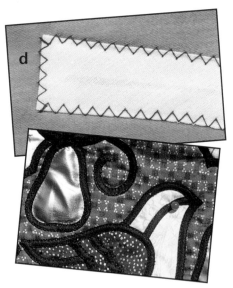

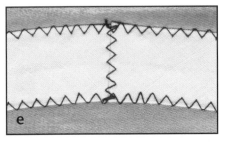

Stitching on the binding

Now, I mentioned that you can stitch the binding on by hand or machine. This is mainly just a matter of preference, but also depends on the finished result you're looking for. I'll describe several different ways, then you can decide which one you like best. So that you can see clearly what's going on, I've done some outsize samples with a wide bias binding; I've also used black thread and very large stitches on a pale binding so that you can see exactly how the stitching looks. Obviously, you'll usually be using a thread that matches your binding – unless you deliberately want a contrast – and your stitching will usually be rather finer!

If you like to stitch by hand, use whatever stitch and stitching technique you would usually use for hand appliqué. I tend to use a slipstitch, working along the bottom of the work, but you may prefer to work along the top line first; do whatever you feel comfortable with. In the finished outsize sample, there's a line of evenly-spaced slipstitches along each edge of the bias binding (**a**).

If you prefer to stitch by machine, set your machine up for a small zigzag – about 1.5 width and 1.5 length. Try a little sample out to see if you're happy with the look of the stitch. Stitch the inside curve first, positioning the zigzag so that most of it is on the binding but the outside edge just overlaps the edge of the binding. Go back to the same end of the binding and stitch the outside of the curve, so that you have a neat line of stitching down each side of the binding (**b**).

Some stitchers like to use the blind hemming stitch on their machine to attach the binding – that's the stitch that makes several straight stitches followed by a V-shape to one side. For this technique, set your machine to the correct stitch; you don't need to use the blind hemming foot – an ordinary zigzag or appliqué foot is fine. Work the stitching so that the straight stitches are just outside the fold of the binding, and the V-shapes are worked into the fold (**c**). With this stitch it isn't possible to work the second edge from the same end as the first, as the stitch is asymmetrical, so you'll need to turn the work round and stitch back along the second edge.

Although this stitch can look more discreet than zigzag, it does mean that quite a large proportion of the stitch is on the fabric patch rather than the binding; this may be a problem if you're using lots of pale fabrics with dark binding, as the dark thread will show on the fabric patches. If you like the look of the blind hemming stitch, you can overcome this problem by using one of the high-quality invisible machine threads.

Neatening ends

Just occasionally, when you're finishing off a stained glass patchwork design, you'll have a raw end of bias binding that you can't lose under a T-junction, so you'll need to know how to neaten it. If the line of the design simply comes to an end, fold the raw edge under neatly, either square or at a slight angle, tuck under any little edges that threaten to creep out, then stitch in place as usual (**d**). I've used this technique in the swirls on the tree in the partridge in a pear tree *(left)*.

If you have to join two raw ends, for instance to complete a circle, it's best not to overlap them as then you end up with one bumpy side and one flat. Instead, fold both edges under as before and butt them up so that they meet exactly; stitch down the join, then stitch the outside edges of the binding using your chosen method (**e**). You'll need this method for the top of the stocking design on page 47.

Occasionally on the designs in this book I've created a pointed end to the bias binding – for example, the end of the olive branch that the dove is holding on page 24. To create a point, pin your line of bias binding on as

usual, then twist the raw end under, pulling it slightly so that you get a smooth curve at the top of the binding line. Pin this twisted section in place. Stitch down the outside edge of the binding as usual until you reach the point (**f**). When you're ready to stitch back along the other edge, cut the excess binding away with very sharp scissors; don't cut the excess away earlier, as the point will fray. Immediately stitch down the point, working a couple of extra stitches if necessary to secure it, then attach the rest of the binding strip (**g**).

Making tight curves

Of course the reason for using bias binding for stained glass patchwork is so that we can use it to cover curved lines; the bias cut allows the strip of binding to take a nice smooth curve. If the curve is quite tight, or if your bias binding is quite firm, hold it in a curve and press it with a steam iron; the steam loosens the fibres and allows them to bend more, and as the binding cools you'll find that it's actually set in its new shape. A quick spray of spray starch before you press also helps this process.

If you need a really tight curve, occasionally just pressing might not be enough. A good solution here is to gather the binding slightly so that it creates a tight but even curve. Set your machine to the longest straight stitch that it can do, and work a line of stitching along one edge of the binding, just inside the fold. Pull the top thread up gently to create a gather, and even the gathers out with your fingers. Once the curve is tight enough, pin the binding in place on your fabric and attach in the usual way, by hand or by machine (**h**).

Corners and points

Corners and points are very easy; you just need to make sure that you keep them sharp and well-defined. When you come to a sharp right-angle, you can either fold the binding so that it creates a straight fold, or mitre it, which is slightly trickier but looks neater. Make your fold, check that it's nice and sharp and straight, then carry on round the design.

Points are created in the same way, either with a straight fold, or mitring the fold so that it goes right down the middle of the point. Again I've done some oversize samples so that you can see those corners and points more clearly; a mitred corner (**i**) and a straight-folded one (**j**), and a mitred point (**k**) and a straight-folded one (**l**).

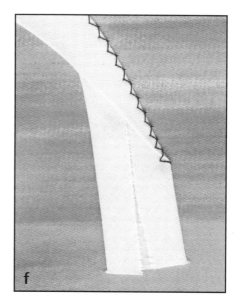

f

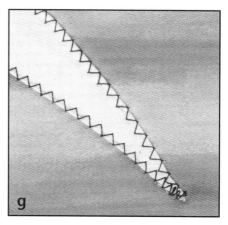

g

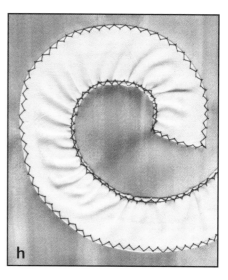

h

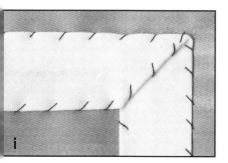

i

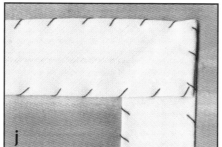

j

k

l

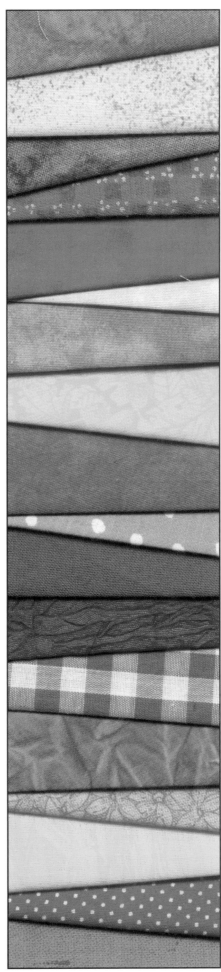

FABRICS

Stitchers today have the most fabulous range of fabrics to choose from – no wonder our fabric stashes are so enormous! If you're new to stained glass patchwork, or if you prefer working in cottons, just stick to those; all the projects in this book can be created very successfully in cotton fabrics. Christmas designs in particular lend themselves to all kinds of other exotic fabrics too, though; further on in this section we'll have a look at some of the options, and how to deal with slightly trickier fabrics such as silks, satins and metallics.

Cottons

There are all kinds of wonderful Christmas-print cotton fabrics on the market; some of these have subtle all-over prints; others are big, splashy novelty prints. I've gathered a collection of Christmas prints together in the samples *(far left)*, and you'll be able to find lots more – or you may already have them in your cupboard …

If you plan to do lots of Christmassy projects, it's also worthwhile collecting a range of basic shades, mottled plains and all-over prints *(centre left)* which will tone well with the seasonal prints, in a selection of greens, reds, blues and golden yellows. These fabrics create good contrasts to the stronger festive prints – and are also often cheaper; use them when you need large pieces for backings, bindings, backgrounds etc.

Exotics *(near left)* are not specifically Christmassy, but their unusual or striking prints or patterns lend themselves well to seasonal projects. Use them relatively sparingly so that you don't overwhelm the designs; I've used them in things like the wise men on page 37, and the background for the angel on page 32.

Silks

Silk fabrics work wonderfully with stained glass patchwork; the sheen on the fabrics makes them glow when they're outlined with bias binding. I've experimented with various kinds of silk, and I've found that dupion *(right)* works best; it's firmer and slightly thicker than some other woven silks, and it's not too sheer. Like most other silk fabrics, though, it does fray badly, so I've developed a way of using it in stained glass patchwork that minimises the problem of fraying.

Draw out your full-size pattern and cut it up to use as templates in the usual way. Instead of cutting the silk exactly along the edge of the template, add a couple of millimetres – maybe a very scant quarter of an inch – outside the template (**a**). You don't need to be exact; you're not actually adding a seam allowance, you're just giving yourself a little overlap.

Lay the patches on your wadding or foundation fabric; you'll find that they overlap slightly. Fidget them around so that the patches and the overlaps look even; if you have a choice, lay a darker fabric over any lighter ones to avoid darker fabrics showing through on the surface. Pin them in position, then stitch a medium-width zigzag along the raw edges between the patches. Begin with the T-junctions, then work your way through the longer lines.

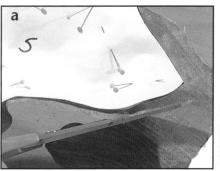

This stitching secures the raw edges and stops them from fraying while you're working; it also means that the patches can't slowly fray and pull out from under the binding after the piece is completed. An extra bonus is that the zigzagging holds all the patches in place while you add the binding. Once all the patches are secure, you can go on and add your bias binding just as usual. This is a technique which you can use for other slippery fabrics such as satin, too; it also works well for very large projects, when you don't want the entire piece covered with pins but don't want to have to tack all the patches!

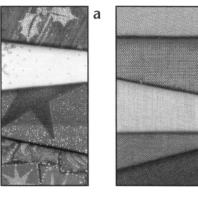

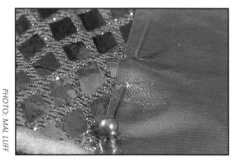

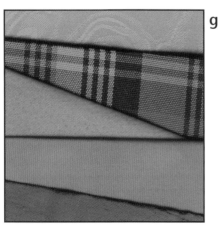

Metallics

As you know if you've seen any of my work, I love using glitzy metallic fabrics – and these look particularly spectacular when they're combined with stained glass patchwork, especially for Christmas projects. I've created the Bethlehem scene on page 34 entirely in metallics. There are many different kinds available these days, and happily many quilt suppliers are stocking them, so if you've been dying to try them, now's the time to branch out! Many people are wary of using metallic fabrics, though, because they seem so very different from using cottons. Won't they melt and stick to the iron? Don't they fray terribly? It's true that metallic fabrics do behave a bit differently from cottons, but in this section I'll show you some tips for getting the best out of metallics.

First of all, if you're using cotton fabrics decorated with metallic prints (**a**), or cottons woven with a smattering of metallic thread (**b**), you treat them just the same way as ordinary cottons. You'll find that you can press them, cut them, piece them and quilt them just as you do classic cotton patchwork fabrics.

Bonded metallic fabrics (**c**) are my favourites, because they're very easy to use and very good-natured. They don't fray, and many of them can be ironed on either the right side or the wrong side – do try a tiny sample out first, though, because they do vary in this! Bonded metallics are occasionally a bit stretchy, as they're manufactured for things like swimsuits and dance costumes; if the one you want to use is a bit floppy, give it a spray of spray starch, then press it, to give it some body.

Some of the bonded metallics have a surface almost like foil (**d**); if you pin through some of these very shiny ones the pins can leave permanent little holes. Just make sure that you pin any patterns on at the very edges, where any stray holes will be covered later by the bias binding, and do the same when you're pinning your patches onto your backing *(left)*.

Lamés (**e**) look lovely but fray very badly; I still use them in my work, because they come in a wonderful range of colours, but I get over the fraying problem by backing the fabrics with lightweight iron-on interfacing.

Some metallic fabrics are covered in shaped and coloured sequins (**f**) – and if you've ever accidentally put an iron on a sequin, you'll know that the sequins melt, and also come unstuck. So, if you're going to use this kind of fabric successfully, you need a thick protective layer, such as a Teflon sheet, between the fabric and the iron – and use the lowest heat for the shortest time that's practical.

As you explore the world of metallic fabrics, you'll find many other types; just cut little samples and experiment with them till you find the best way of working with that particular fabric. And if you're doing a whole project in metallic fabrics, you might find it helpful to use the same method that I showed you for working with silk (see page 7); cut all the patches a little bit bigger than the templates, and zigzag them all in place on a foundation fabric before you begin adding the binding.

Other challenging fabrics

Because of the way the technique works, you really can use virtually any fabric for stained glass patchwork, but some fabrics present particular challenges, and it's worth knowing some tips to help you get the very best out of them. In this section we'll look at fabrics which have a pile or heavy texture, fabrics which fray badly, satins and other slippery customers, and sheer fabrics and lace.

Many synthetic fabrics (**g**) are firm, closely-woven and stable, and don't need any special handling at all; I've used lots of fabrics like these ones in stained glass patchwork projects.

Some fabrics have a pile or heavy texture, such as velvets, corduroys, fur fabrics and thick laces (**h**); if you put a hot iron straight onto these fabrics, you can flatten the texture and spoil their look. Instead, lay the fabric right side down on a small towel and press from the back *(far right)*; the towelling cushions the pile or the texture of the fabric so that you can press it without spoiling it.

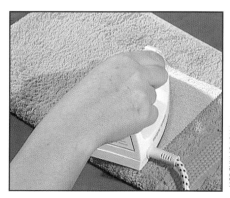

Sheer fabrics can have a lovely sheen but are too fine to use just as they are for stained glass patchwork; when I'm using fabrics like this, I give them extra body by adding a layer of lightweight iron-on interfacing.

Some heavy woven fabrics (**i**) fray badly, but if they're already quite thick you don't want to add any thickness by using interfacing. Reduce the fraying problem by working a stabilising line of zigzag stitching round the edges of the patch; cut out the shape, slightly outside the stitching *(far right)*, and your patch is ready to use.

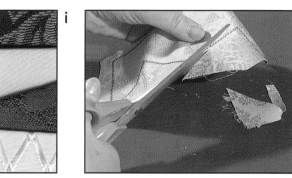

Nets and laces often have attractive patterns woven into them, but they are too sheer to use as they are in stained glass patchwork because they show too much of the background. Overcome this problem by layering them with another fabric; pin the two layers together, and either cut your patch out from the double fabric, or zigzag round the shape of the patch and then cut out the shape just outside the stitching line *(right)*.

Satins (**j**) have a beautiful sheen which I like exploiting in stained glass patchwork, but they are **very** slippery. This can make it tricky to cut accurate patches for stained glass patchwork, but there's an easy way of making the satin more stable. It's called spray starch! Lay your fabric right side down on the ironing board, spray a little starch all across the fabric, then iron it; this gives you a much more stable fabric which you can then cut more accurately. Do try the starch out on a small sample first, though; on a few fabrics it might leave a slight watermark – in which case you could try backing the satin with iron-on interfacing instead.

BIAS BINDINGS (AND ALTERNATIVES ...)

Now let's talk about bias bindings. When I'm demonstrating stained glass patchwork, the question I'm asked most often is whether I make my own bias binding. The answer is that I very rarely bother. I've found that lots of people have been put off the technique by spending hours cutting strips and folding under the edges; my theory is that there are machines that can do that: let's get on with creative bit!

Picking a good binding

Do buy good-quality bias binding, though; the stuff you can buy in markets is cheap, but is often quite poor quality. Ordinary haberdasher's binding is colour-fast, well-woven, washable, and shrink-proof; it also comes in lots of different colours, widths, and fabrics, such as cotton, cotton/polyester mixes, satin and metallic. Of course, if you enjoy making your own binding (some people find it soothing), then of course please do – and you may well find that it's cheaper.

The widths I most often use are:

• the standard ⅓-½in wide (10-12mm), which is useful for simple designs and medium-to-large items (I've used it for the dove on page 24, the window scene on page 41, and the stars on pages 26 and 28).

• ¼in wide (5-6mm); this is excellent for more detailed designs, such as the angel (page 32), the Christmas tree on page 23, and the candle on page 13.

Many of the projects in this book use the traditional black bias binding, but of course you don't have to use black; just make sure that you have a good contrast to the colours in your patches, so that you can see the lines of the design. For the large star on page 28 I've used royal blue binding, and for the stocking on page 39 I've used red-brown.

Fusible binding

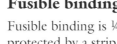

Fusible binding is ¼in wide, and has a little strip of bonding web on the back, protected by a strip of paper; when you're ready to use it, you peel off the paper (**a**), lay the binding in position over your line, and fuse it into place with a warm iron (**b**), which holds it in position while you stitch. Why might you want to use fusible binding, though? And what's the point of making it fusible, if you still have to stitch it in place?

First of all, you've got a ready-made narrow bias binding which is perfect for more detailed stained glass patchwork designs where you want a slightly finer line. Because the raw edges are folded under, instead of seamed, it also isn't too bulky. And being fusible, this binding eliminates any need to pin or tack; as you press it in place it takes a beautiful curve, which it holds perfectly while you stitch it by hand or machine. Also, the bonding web helps to hold the raw edges of the fabric patches in place, which is a bonus if you're using narrow binding.

The fusible binding also comes in loads of different colours, including a whole range of metallic finishes, and the multicoloured version I've used for the Christmas tree on page 21. Fusible binding is more expensive than other types of narrow binding, but it is easy to use and very striking.

If you want a fusible binding in a particular colour or finish and can't get hold of what you're looking for, many quilt suppliers now sell bonding web in thin strips for making your own. Peel off a section of the web strip, lay it web side down on the back of your binding, and fuse it into place. Some suppliers are also selling a gadget which adds a fusible strip to your own home-made binding as you create it.

Working with straight lines

So far we've been looking at using bias binding for creating the lines of the stained glass patchwork designs, but you only need to use bias binding when the design has curves in it. If your design is completely made up of straight lines, like the large star on page 28, there are all kind of alternatives you can use. This is your chance to try out ribbons, braids, strips of fabric, seam binding tape, petersham, broderie anglaise, lace – anything that will create an attractive line. On the heart decorations on page 19, I've used broderie anglaise laced with red ribbon, and plain wide gold ribbon. This variation of the basic stained glass patchwork technique opens up all kinds of exciting possibilities!

QUILTING

As quilters, we don't just want to do piecing and appliqué, we want to live up to our name: we want to quilt our work too! One of the many things I like about stained glass patchwork is that, if you want, you can quilt the work as you go. Of course, if you prefer, you can quilt it afterwards, by hand or machine – see below – but first of all I'll explain how you can combine the stained glass patchwork and the quilting in one process.

Waddings

These days there are almost as many kinds of wadding around as there are fabrics. Don't let them confuse you; if you're not sure what kind of wadding to use, pick one that you've tried and liked before, or use a basic 2oz polyester wadding that is a good all-purpose wadding. If you use quite a squashy wadding like the 2oz, it's best to use a backing of muslin or some other fabric to make a complete three-layer sandwich; the three layers pulling together as you stitch them creates a good quilted look. If you use one of the flatter waddings such as firm cotton ones, or the more compact polyester waddings I particularly like, you won't necessarily need a muslin backing – try it with and without, and see what you prefer. I'm a great believer that the best quilting technique for you is often simply what you feel most comfortable doing.

Quilting as you go

1. If you're using a muslin backing, lay this down on a flat surface and smooth it out; cover it with the wadding, then lay your foundation fabric, with its tracing, on top of the wadding. Now cut out your fabric patches in the usual way, lay them in place and pin them in position.

2. If you prefer, you can stitch while the layers are pinned together, but if it's a large piece of work it's often easier to tack the layers together. Tacking holds the three layers in their proper positions and stops them from slithering about and distorting while you're quilting – if you don't like tacking you can use safety pins at regular intervals, or a tack gun that shoots little plastic tags through the layers, or you can use one of the spray glues that are sold specially for quilt use.

3. Now add the bias binding in exactly the same way as for the basic technique – beginning with the T-junctions and working your way through the design. The only difference is that now, as you stitch on the bias binding by hand or by machine, you're quilting as you stitch. I used this method for the harlequin Christmas tree (**a**), and the poinsettia (**b**).

Quilting completed designs

You may prefer to quilt your project, by hand or machine, or to add more texture, **after** you've added the binding. If you want to quilt in this way, the world is your oyster; you can use virtually any hand or machine quilting technique on stained glass patchwork projects, but here I'll show you just a couple of ideas to get you started.

* On the lap quilt (**c**) I've used big-stitch quilting to outline each patch, roughly ¼in inside each seam.

* Free-machine-quilted stars echo the theme of the large star panel (**d**); the curvy quilted design creates a nice counterpoint to the straight lines of the patches.

a

b

c

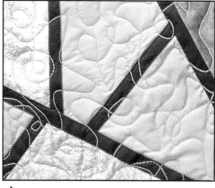

d

e

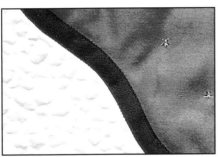

f

g

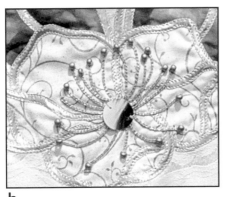

h

❊ Wavy lines of machine quilting (**e**) radiate outwards from the dove in the centre of the design on page 24. You can use a special walking foot for machine quilting, but for small projects and simple lines like this you don't really need one.

❊ Vermicelli or stipple stitching is a popular way of adding texture by machine (**f**); I've used it on the snow parts of the window panel on page 41.

EMBELLISHING

Another way you can add visual interest is by embellishing your work with beads, buttons, charms, sequins and fabric paints – go to any quilt show and you'll find more ideas than you could use in a lifetime! How you decorate your quilt will depend very much on the finished effect you're looking for, but in this section I'll just show you a few ideas that I've used on the projects in this book.

❊ Brightly-coloured plastic beads stitched onto the gingerbread house (see page 52) create the impression of sweets and candies (**g**).

❊ In the centre of the Christmas rose, I've couched down gold threads and finished each one with a gold bead to make the stamens (**h**).

❊ Beads and hand embroidery (**i**) give a rich crazy patchwork feel to the blue-and-gold heart (see page 19).

❊ Little mirrors, or shisha (**j**), look effective scattered across the harlequin Christmas tree (see page 21).

❊ Use Christmas charms, beads and trimmings to decorate your own stitched tree (**k**).

And, of course, you'll think of many other ways of embellishing your own seasonal stained glass projects; there are hundreds of specifically Christmassy buttons, beads and charms on the market, such as angels, stockings, candy sticks, reindeer, Santas, baubles and even Christmas tree lights …

i

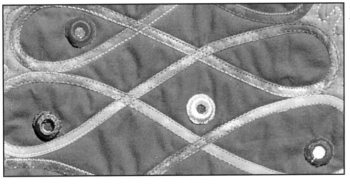

j   k

The Projects

✪ DECK THE HALLS ✪

Candle picture

Candles are a popular part of any Christmas; this design gives you the chance to create your own everlasting candle decoration in stained glass patchwork. If you use silks and satins for the candle flame and surround, they'll catch the light and reflect it – the effect is enhanced by the lines of gold bias binding.

FINISHED SIZE: 17 x 24in (43 x 61cm)

EASINESS RATING: Easy to medium; the cutting and stitching of the design is straightforward. If you use satins and silks, as I have, use the technique described for working with silk (see page 7) to minimise fraying.

STITCHING TIP: *When you're creating the border, make sure that you fold the blue and gold fabric so that you're marking the wrong side. This way, it doesn't matter if you make a mistake while you're drawing the arched shape.*

You will need

- 17 x 24in (43 x 61cm) blue and gold fabric for the border
- 20 x 13in (50 x 33cm) white or cream fabric for the background
- 17 x 24in (43 x 61cm) compressed wadding
- 18 x 25in (45 x 63cm) plain red fabric for the backing and binding
- 7 x 5in (18 x 13cm) red and gold print fabric for the candle
- 8in (20cm) squares of bright yellow and pale orange fabrics for the flame surrounds
- 5in (13cm) square of bright orange fabric for the flame
- 4in (10cm) square of bright red fabric for the flame centre
- 6in (15cm) square of bright green fabric for the holly leaves
- two large red beads for the holly berries
- 2½yd (2.5m) gold bias binding, ¼in (6mm) wide
- 7yd (7m) black bias binding, ¼in (6mm) wide
- 2yd (2m) metallic green bias binding, ¼in (6mm) wide
- black, green, red and yellow or gold sewing threads
- soft pencil, chalk marker
- extra fabric for a hanging sleeve, or ribbon or tape for display loops

Instructions

Trace or photocopy the candle design from pages 58-59. Lay the white or cream fabric over the design and trace all the solid lines in pencil.

Cut up the design along the solid lines and use the pieces as templates to cut patches from the appropriate fabrics, remembering to lay the templates right side up on the right side of the fabric. As you cut each fabric patch, add about ⅛in (1-2mm) extra all round the edge, just to give you a small overlap when you lay the pieces down.

3 Pin the patches in position on the background fabric, and stitch round the outlines with a small zigzag to secure the patches.

4 In pencil, draw extra lines on the patches to correspond to the dotted lines on the design; these don't need to be too exact. Lay the wadding on a flat surface and position the design on top, right side up; pin or tack the layers together.

5 You're now ready to add the bias binding; follow the sequence shown (**a**) to add the lines around the candle, flame and holly leaves in the correct order. (Note that some of the lines of binding are black and some are gold.)

a

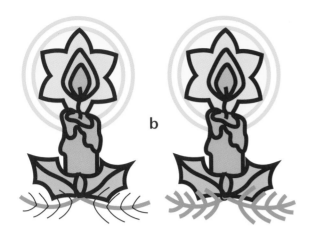

b

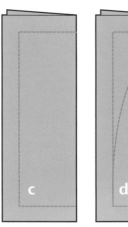

c

d

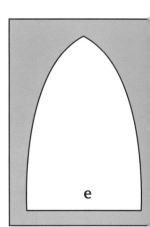

e

6 Follow the sequence shown (**b**) to create the sprigs of greenery; fold the raw ends of the binding lines under to neaten them.

7 Fold the rectangle of blue and gold fabric in half down its length, right sides together. Measure in 3in (8cm) from the top and bottom and the raw edge, and draw lines in chalk (**c**); then draw a smooth curved line from the centre top point to the bottom corner of the chalk line (**d**). When you're happy with the shape, cut along the marked line to create an arched shape when the fabric is unfolded (**e**); press out the crease.

8 Lay the arched shape over the candle design and stitch a line of small zigzag round the arched shape; cover this with a line of black bias binding.

9 Lay the plain red fabric right side down on a flat surface and position the design, right side up, on top so that there is an even border of red fabric all the way around. Fold the raw edges to the front of the work to create an even binding and secure them with a line of small zigzag; cover the stitching line with a line of black bias binding.

10 Use red thread to stitch on the berries between the holly leaves, then add a hanging sleeve on the back, or display loops of tape or ribbon.

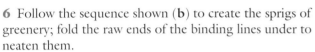

❂ DECK THE HALLS ❂

Christmas Greenery

Make your table look really festive and ready for that Christmas dinner with seasonal leaves and flowers created in stained glass patchwork. I've used a Christmas rose, or hellebore, to decorate a ready-made table runner, and the traditional holly and ivy for a padded breadcloth, for keeping rolls warm at the table.

FINISHED SIZE:
table runner: the design measures 10 x 8in (25 x 20cm)
breadcloth: 18in (45cm) square

EASINESS RATING: Fairly easy, as the designs are small and not too complex. If you're an absolute beginner, try the breadcloth first.

STITCHING TIP: *If you can't find a table runner like the one I've used, just cut a long strip of damask cloth instead, and either shape the ends into points or leave them plain. For the breadcloth, I bought two damask table napkins instead of cutting my own squares.*

You will need

For the table runner:

* cream damask table runner, or strip of cream damask fabric at least 13in (33cm) wide
* 8 x 5in (20 x 13cm) gold and cream print fabric for the flower
* 10 x 5in (25 x 13cm) green mottled or print fabric for the leaves
* gold embroidery thread, gold beads and one large gold sequin for the flower centre
* 3yd (3m) of gold bias binding, ¼in (6mm) wide
* gold or cream sewing thread
* soft pencil

For the breadcloth:

* two 18in (45cm) squares of cream damask
* 18in (45cm) square of compressed wadding
* 7in (18cm) square green mottled fabric for the ivy leaf
* 6in (15cm) square green print fabric for the holly leaves
* 5in (13cm) square white organza or tulle for the centre of the ivy leaf
* two large gold beads
* 3yd (3m) of gold bias binding, ¼in (6mm) wide
* 2½yd (2.5m) of gold bias binding, 1in (2.5cm) wide
* gold or cream sewing thread
* soft pencil

Instructions

To make the table runner:

1 Trace or photocopy the design on page 60. Lay the end of the table runner over the design, right side up, and use a pencil to trace the solid outlines of the design onto the runner.

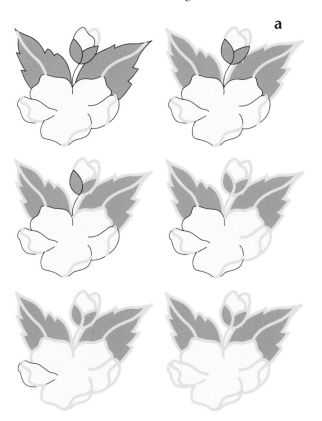

a

2 Cut up the paper design along the solid lines, and use the shapes as templates to cut two leaf shapes and the bottom of the bud from the green fabric, and a flower and a bud from the gold print. Lay these patches in position over the drawing on the table runner and pin them in place; you may find it useful to secure them in position with a small zigzag if the damask is slippery. Now use pencil to draw in the dotted lines shown on the pattern.

3 Add the lines of bias binding in order, stitching by hand or by machine and following the sequence shown in the diagrams below left (**a**).

4 Once all the bias binding is in place, embroider or couch curved lines of gold embroidery thread out from the centre of the flower to suggest stamens. Stitch a gold bead onto the end of each stamen, then stitch the gold sequin in the centre of the flower.

to make the breadcloth:

1 Trace or photocopy the design on page 61. Take one of the squares of damask and lay one corner over the design, right side up, so that the design is about 2in (5cm) in from the sides. Use pencil to trace the solid outlines of the design onto the fabric.

2 Cut up the paper design along the solid lines, and use the shapes as templates. Cut two holly leaves from the print fabric. Use the ivy template to cut one whole ivy leaf from the mottled green, then cut along the dotted line and use the inner shape to cut a patch from the organza. Pin the holly and the green ivy leaf in position on the damask, then pin the organza shape in position on top of the ivy leaf. Go round all the edges of the patches with a small zigzag to secure them.

b

3 Lay the second square of damask on a flat surface, right side down, and cover it with the square of wadding. Position the design, right side up, on top, and pin the layers together. Now add the lines of bias binding in order, stitching by hand or by machine and following the sequence shown (**b**).

4 Use large fabric scissors to round off the corners of the squares evenly. Bind the edge of the breadcloth all the way round with the wider bias binding, positioning the join at the opposite corner to the design. Stitch on the gold beads as holly berries to complete the design.

✪ DECK THE HALLS ✪

Poinsettia & Partridge

Two pretty seasonal motifs – a scarlet poinsettia, set off by rich green foliage, and a partridge in a pear tree. These two designs look good together, as they're similar proportions and made in the same way, but of course you can do them individually. Or, if you're feeling ambitious, turn to pages 106 onwards for the other 11 days of Christmas, and stitch the set!

FINISHED SIZE: each hanging measures 16 x 21in (41 x 53cm)

EASINESS RATING: Medium; good first stained glass projects for confident stitchers. If you're new to quilting, try these designs when you've practised on a couple of easier ones.

STITCHING TIP: *Fusible binding is useful for these designs, as it saves pinning or tacking the curves and corners.*

You will need

for the poinsettia:
❋ 9½ x 14in (24 x 35cm) Christmas print fabric for the background
❋ 16 x 21in (41 x 53cm) gold and cream print fabric for the border
❋ 18 x 23in (45 x 57cm) black fabric for the backing and binding
❋ 12in (30cm) square of mottled red fabric for the flower
❋ 12 x 8in (30 x 20cm) green print fabric for leaves

❋ 12 x 8in (30 x 20cm) plain green fabric for leaves
❋ 8yd (8m) black bias binding, ¼in (6mm) wide
❋ black and cream sewing threads; compressed wadding
❋ six large gold teardrop-shaped beads
❋ soft pencil

for the partridge:
❋ 9½ x 14in (24 x 35cm) gold and cream print fabric for the background
❋ 16 x 21in (41 x 53cm) Christmas print fabric for the border
❋ 18 x 23in (45 x 57cm) black fabric for the backing and binding
❋ 10in (25cm) square of green print fabric for the tree
❋ 5in (13cm) square of red and gold print for the wing
❋ 5in (13cm) square of red and gold striped fabric for the pot
❋ 5in (13cm) square of bonded gold fabric for the pears
❋ large scraps of plain green, plain red, mid brown, pale yellow and mid yellow fabric
❋ 7yd (7m) black bias binding, ¼in (6mm) wide
❋ black and red sewing threads; compressed wadding
❋ small round red or brown bead for the partridge's eye
❋ soft pencil

Instructions

to make the poinsettia:

1 Trace or photocopy the design on pages 62-63. Lay the background fabric over the design, right side up, and use a pencil to trace the solid outlines only of the design onto the fabric. Cut up the paper design along the solid lines, and discard the background section to leave you with a border, a flower shape and six leaves.

Use the pattern pieces as templates to cut your fabric patches, laying them right side up on the right side of the fabric. When you cut the border, use the template just for cutting out the inner rectangle of the fabric, so that you have a wider fabric border than your paper template. Pin the patches in position over the drawing on the background fabric; once the whole design is assembled, go round all the outlines with a small zigzag to secure the patches. On the flower shape and the leaves, use pencil to draw in the dotted lines shown on the pattern – you don't need to be too accurate about these lines, so you can just copy them by eye.

Lay the wadding on a flat surface and pin the design on top, right side up. Add the lines of bias binding in order, stitching by hand or by machine and following the sequence shown in the diagrams below.

Once all the bias binding is in place, attach the gold beads radiating from the centre of the flower.

5 Lay the black backing fabric on a flat surface, right side down, and position the flower design on top so that there's an even border of fabric all the way around. Fold the raw edges over to the front in a narrow double hem, and stitch down the fold by hand or machine. Add a hanging sleeve or display loops to complete the design.

to make the partridge:

1 Trace or photocopy the design on pages 64-65. Lay the background fabric over the design, right side up, and use a pencil to trace the solid outlines only of the design onto the fabric. Cut up the paper design along the solid lines, and discard the background section to leave you with a border and assorted smaller pieces.

2 Use the pattern pieces as templates to cut your fabric patches, laying them right side up on the right side of the fabric. When you cut the border, use the template just for cutting out the inner rectangle of the fabric, so that you have a wider fabric border than your paper template. Pin the patches in position over the drawing on the background fabric; once the whole design is assembled, go round all the outlines with a small zigzag to secure the patches. On the tree, pot and wing shapes, use pencil to draw in the dotted lines shown on the pattern – you don't need to be too accurate about these lines, so you can just copy them by eye.

3 Lay the wadding on a flat surface and pin the design on top, right side up. Add the lines of bias binding in order, stitching by hand or by machine and following the sequence shown in the diagrams below. Once all the bias binding is in place, stitch the bead in position to create the partridge's eye.

4 Lay the black backing fabric on a flat surface, right side down, and position the design on top so that there's an even border of fabric all the way around. Fold the raw edges over to the front in a narrow double hem, and stitch down the fold by hand or machine. Add a hanging sleeve or display loops to complete the design.

THE PROJECTS: DECK THE HALLS

✪ DECK THE HALLS ✪

Crazy Christmas Hearts

Believe it or not, these two very different heart decorations are made from exactly the same pattern, both using a combination of stained glass patchwork and crazy patchwork. The red, green and white heart uses folk plaids and broderie anglaise for a country feel, while the blue and gold heart has echoes of Indian textiles with its exotic fabrics and rich embellishment.

FINISHED SIZE: the red, green and white heart is 13 x 15in (33 x 38cm) the blue and gold heart is 11 x 14in (28 x 36cm)

EASINESS RATING: Very easy; perfect starter projects if you're new to stained glass patchwork.

STITCHING TIP: *The blue and gold heart can be as simple or as complex as you wish; if you're feeling ambitious, encrust it with hand embroidery and beads or add some shisha (see page 21).*

You will need

for the red, green and white heart:
- ❋ five 8in (20cm) squares of fabrics in toning red, green and white plains, prints and plaids
- ❋ 12in (30cm) square of compressed wadding
- ❋ 12in (30cm) square of plain red or green fabric for the backing

- ❋ 1yd (1m) broderie anglaise with eyelets for threading
- ❋ 1yd (1m) fine red or green ribbon for threading the broderie anglaise
- ❋ 1½yd (1.5m) gathered broderie anglaise for the ruffle
- ❋ 9in (23cm) red ribbon or cord for the hanging loop
- ❋ 1yd (1m) white bias binding, ½in (12mm) wide
- ❋ wide green ribbon bow
- ❋ white and green sewing threads

for the blue and gold heart:
- ❋ five 8in (20cm) squares of exotic fabrics in toning blue and gold prints and plains
- ❋ 12in (30cm) square of compressed wadding
- ❋ 12in (30cm) square of plain blue fabric for the backing
- ❋ 1yd (1m) gold ribbon, ¾in (2cm) wide
- ❋ 1yd (1m) gold bias binding, 1in (2.5cm) wide
- ❋ 9in (23cm) gold or blue ribbon or cord for the hanging loop
- ❋ gold and blue sewing threads
- ❋ assorted blue and gold embroidery threads and beads for embellishment

Instructions

to make the red, green and white heart:

1 Trace or photocopy templates **A**, **B**, **C**, **D** and **E** from pages 66-67; cut the shapes out and use them as templates to cut five fabric patches, laying them right side up on the right side of the fabric.

5 Fold the hanging cord or ribbon into a loop and stitch it behind the centre top of the heart; add a line of bias binding on the back of the heart to enclose all the raw edges and the ends of the hanging loop. Stitch the green heart to the centre top to complete the decoration.

to make the blue and gold heart:

1 Create the heart shape from the different fabrics and wadding as described in steps 1 and 2 (above). Following the sequence shown in the diagram below, add lengths of gold ribbon to cover the joins between the patches.

2 Bind the raw edges of the heart shape with the gold bias binding, beginning and ending at the centre top; before you neaten the ends of the binding where they join, fold the hanging loop in half, slip the raw ends under the binding on the back of the heart, then seal these raw ends in as you finish off the binding.

3 If you wish, decorate some of the lines of gold ribbon with embroidery stitches and beads; I've used herringbone stitch, and single and double feather stitches. You might also like to add scatterings of beads across one or more of the fabric patches.

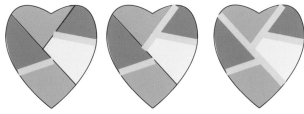

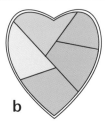

a

2 Lay the square of backing fabric on a flat surface, right side down, and cover with the square of wadding. Lay the patches in position on top to create a heart shape (**a**), and pin in place. Trim the backing and wadding to the heart shape (**b**).

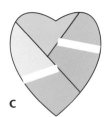

b

3 Thread the fine ribbon through the eyelets in the flat broderie anglaise. Cut lengths to fit the joins between the patches and stitch them in place on the heart shape, by hand or machine, following the sequence shown (**c**).

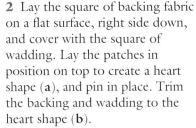

c

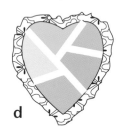

d

4 Stitch the gathered broderie anglaise round the edge of the heart shape to cover the raw edges (**d**); make a pleat in the ruffle at the bottom of the heart to help it lie flat at the point. Tuck the raw ends under where they join at the top.

Harlequin Christmas Tree

Random-dyed bias binding and simple quilting in multicoloured thread make something special out of a very simple design. I've embellished this tree with shisha (little mirrors) and an appliquéd star, but you could add all kinds of bits and pieces of your own.

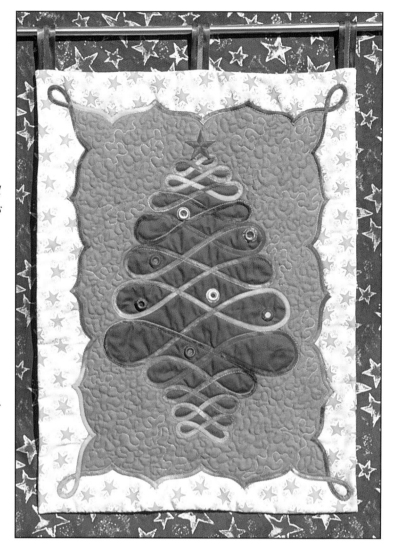

FINISHED SIZE: 17 x 22in (43 x 56cm)

EASINESS RATING: The stained glass patchwork is **quick and easy**, as there's only one fabric patch to cut and one long line of binding to attach. If you're not confident with the free machine quilting I've used for the background, leave it out; other ways of making the design simpler are to add a plain border rather than the shaped one I've used, and to omit the fancy hanging loops.

STITCHING TIP: *I've used ready-woven shisha surrounds, which come in assorted colours along with foil 'mirrors' to go underneath, but if you're familiar with the technique you can embroider your own surrounds for real shisha – little circles cut from mirror glass.*

You will need

❋ two 18 x 23in (45 x 24cm) rectangles of plain green fabric for the background and the backing
❋ 18 x 23in (45 x 24cm) Christmas print fabric for the border
❋ 18 x 23in (45 x 24cm) compressed 2oz wadding
❋ 12 x 16in (30 x 41cm) rich green fabric for the tree
❋ 18in (45cm) green ribbon, 1in (2.5cm) wide, for the hanging loops
❋ 7yd (7m) of multicoloured fusible bias binding, ¼in (6mm) wide
❋ multicoloured sewing thread
❋ assorted small shisha mirrors and their surrounds, plus toning thread
❋ ready-embroidered star
❋ soft pencil, chalk marker

Instructions

1 Trace or photocopy the tree shape (**A**) on pages 68-69, and trace it in pencil onto your green tree fabric (you might need the help of a lightbox or a bright window for this). Cut just round the outside of the shape, and pin it onto one of the green rectangles; stitch a line of small zigzag round just the outside of the shape to secure it (**a**).

2 Trace or photocopy the curved shape (**B**) on page 68 and cut it out. Measure in 2in (5cm) from each edge of the green rectangle and draw a line in chalk marker (**b**); lay the paper shape along this line and draw three repeats of it along the top and bottom edge, and four repeats down each side (**c**), making sure that the sides are even. Add a loop at each corner (**d**).

3 Lay the border fabric on a flat surface, right side up, and cover it with the green rectangle, right side up. Pin the layers together, then stitch a small zigzag round the curved line marked on the green fabric. Cut away the excess background fabric fabric just **outside** the zigzag line to reveal the border fabric (**e**). On the back of the work, cut away the excess border fabric just **inside** the zigzag.

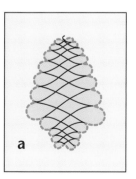

a

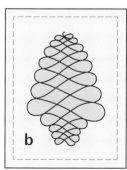

b

c

d

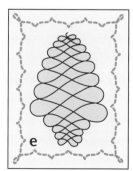

e

4 Now it's time to add the bias binding. The tree shape is created with a single line; use the tip of a warm iron to fuse it in place, starting at the top of the tree and working down to the bottom of the pot. Tuck the final raw end under the loop just above it to neaten it (you don't need to neaten the top end as it will be hidden by the star). Add a second line of binding round the curved line of the border.

5 Lay the wadding out on a flat surface and position the design, right side up, on top. Secure the two layers using your preferred method (tacking, safety pins, quilt glue, tack gun etc).

6 Thread your machine with multicoloured thread, and stitch a small zigzag down each edge of each line of binding round the tree; don't worry that the lines of stitching cross each other where the binding creates loops. (Don't stitch the binding round the border just yet.) Drop the feed dogs, put the embroidery foot on the machine, and work a vermicelli stitch across the green background area.

7 Fuse a line of bias binding down the centre of the green ribbon, and stitch in place with a small zigzag. Cut the ribbon into three 6in (15cm) lengths, and fold each length in half, wrong sides together.

8 Put the tree design right sides together with the remaining rectangle of green fabric; insert the hanging loops between the layers at even intervals along the top edge, positioning them so that the raw edges align. Stitch a

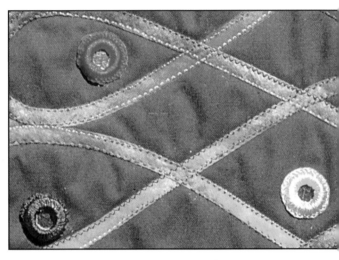

½in (12mm) seam all round the edges of the rectangle, leaving about 6in (15cm) open along the bottom edge for turning. Trim the seams, clip the corners, and turn the piece right side out; press just the very edges of the panel so that you don't squash the wadding.

9 Turn in the raw edges of the opening and slipstitch them closed. Finally, work a small zigzag round the edges of the remaining line of binding to secure it in place and to keep the layers together.

10 Stitch the star in place at the top of the tree, then stitch the shishas across the design.

✪ DECK THE HALLS ✪

Embellished Christmas Tree

This little tree panel is great as a decoration or as a present! You can embellish the finished wall-hanging with beads, braid, little baubles, Christmas charms etc to personalise it; I've added lines of gold and silver beading to look like loops of tinsel.

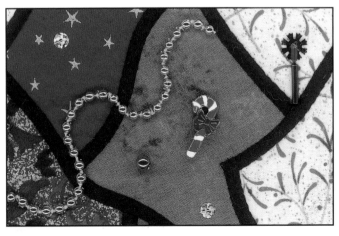

FINISHED SIZE: 16 x 21in (41 x 53cm)

EASINESS RATING: Fairly easy; a good project for the confident beginner. If you're experienced at stained glass patchwork, you'll polish this design off in no time.

STITCHING TIP: *You can use black bias binding for this design, or choose red, green, gold or silver – any colour that contrasts well with your fabrics.*

You will need

※ 18 x 23in (46 x 58cm) black cotton fabric for the backing and outside binding

※ 9½ x 14in (24 x 35cm) white or cream, plain or print fabric for the background

※ 16 x 21in (41 x 53cm) contrasting Christmas print or plain for the border

※ large scraps of several green-based Christmas prints and plains for the tree

※ scrap of red-based print or plain for the tree pot

※ 5yd (5m) of bias binding, ¼in (6mm) wide

※ sewing thread to match the bias binding

※ 16 x 21in (41 x 53cm) 2oz polyester wadding

※ 16 x 21in (41 x 53cm) white or cream muslin

※ short length of black tape or ribbon for the hanging loops, or extra strip of black fabric for a casing

※ pencil, ruler

※ assorted Christmassy beads, little baubles, charms, lace, braid, embroidery threads etc to embellish your design

Instructions

1 Trace or photocopy the tree design on pages 70-71, then lay the background fabric over the design and trace the lines in pencil.

2 Cut up the pattern, and use the shapes as templates to cut patches from your fabrics; pin these in position on the background fabric, and go over the outlines with a small zigzag to keep the patches in place.

3 Lay the border fabric, right side up, on a flat surface, and position the tree design on top so that there's an even border of fabric all the way around. Stitch a line of small zigzag round the very edge of the white or cream fabric. On the back of the work, cut away the excess border fabric, cutting just **inside** the line of zigzag stitches.

4 Lay the wadding on a flat surface and cover with the tree design; now add the lines of bias binding, following the stitching sequence shown below right.

5 Lay the black backing fabric right side down and position the tree design on top so that there's an even border of fabric all the way around; fold the raw edges over to the front of the work in a narrow double hem, and stitch along the fold by hand or machine.

6 Embellish the tree and its surrounds to your heart's content with beads, sequins, lace etc; if you wish, add imitation candles at the tips of the tree as I've done (see opposite). I've also stitched gold snowflake charms on the background and the border (see below). Add a hanging sleeve or display loops to complete the panel.

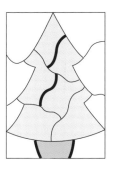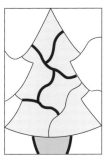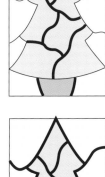

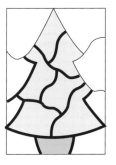

✪ THE CHRISTMAS STORY ✪

Dove & Olive Branch

Holding an olive branch in its beak, this striking dove flies through a royal blue sky. At this size the wall-hanging makes a stunning Christmas centrepiece (it would also work well as a church banner), but if you don't want such a large finished piece, make the design at one-quarter size (see the stitching tip below).

FINISHED SIZE: 40 x 70in (100 x 175cm)

EASINESS RATING: Medium/confident stitcher. Although the design is large, it's not difficult to do. The dove is all one piece of fabric, and so is the background; the design is created through the lines of bias binding. I've kept the quilting very simple, just using lines of wavy machine stitching radiating out from the dove once the bias binding is added.

STITCHING TIP: *If you prefer a smaller version of the dove, use 5in (12.5cm) squares for your grid and ¼in (6mm) binding; this will give you a finished size of 20 x 35in (50 x 87.5cm). Remember to scale down all your fabric and binding requirements accordingly.*

You will need

※ 40 x 70in (100 x 175cm) blue and silver fabric for the background
※ 40 x 70in (100 x 175cm) compressed wadding
※ 43 x 73in (108 x 183cm) plain green fabric for the backing and binding
※ 50 x 25in (130 x 65cm) silver or pale blue fabric for the dove
※ large scraps of mottled green fabric for the olive leaves
※ roughly 30yd (30m) black bias binding, ½in (12mm) wide

※ black, royal blue and white sewing threads
※ pack of dressmaker's tracing paper
※ soft pencil, black felt pen, pale crayon, ruler
※ extra fabric for a hanging sleeve, or ribbon or tape for display loops
※ small, round black bead for the dove's eye

Instructions

1 Tape two or more sheets of dressmaker's tracing paper together to create a rectangle 40 x 70in (100 x 175cm). Divide this into a grid of four squares by seven, each square measuring 10in or 25cm.

2 Use the grid method to enlarge the design on page 72; copy the lines of the design onto your grid, enlarging them as you go, to create a full-size pattern. Begin with the dove and the olive branch, then add lines across the background – don't worry about making these identical to mine. Go over the lines with black felt pen to make them stronger.

3 Lay the blue and silver background fabric, right side up, over the pattern and pin the two layers together firmly. Tape the whole design onto a large window on a sunny day, and trace the solid lines of the design onto the fabric in pale crayon (**a**).

4 Cut out the dove shape and the olive leaf shapes from the paper pattern and discard the rest of the paper. Lay the dove fabric over the dove drawing and trace all the lines – solid and dotted – in pencil. Use the olive leaf shapes as templates to cut five leaves from the mottled green fabric. Lay the leaf and dove patches in position on the background fabric and go round the outlines only with zigzag stitch to hold the patches in place (**b**).

5 You now need to look carefully at your design to work out the T-junctions (see page 2); these will vary slightly depending on exactly where you've drawn your lines, but I've shown the first T-junctions on my design in **c**. Add lines of bias binding along the lines of the design, working your way through the sequence of T-junctions until all the lines are covered. (If you find that you've forgotten one T-junction, simply slit a few stitches and slip the end of the binding underneath.)

6 Once the stained glass patchwork is done, press the design from the back. Lay the green backing fabric right side down on a flat surface and lay the wadding on top; position the dove design, right side up, on top, so that there's an even border of fabric all the way around. Secure the layers using your favourite method (tacking, safety pins, quilt glue, tack gun etc).

7 Thread your machine with the white machine quilting thread and set it to a simple wavy stitch if you have one on your machine (if not, just use a long straight stitch but work it in long wavy lines, or pick a different decorative stitch). Work one line of stitching along each of the dove's feathers, and one line round each other dove section.

8 Re-thread the machine with blue thread, and now work a series of lines of stitching radiating out from the edge of the dove shape to the edge of the blue fabric – like the rays of a sun (**d**).

9 Fold the green fabric over to the front of the work in a double fold and tack it in place; stitch down the folded edge by hand or machine, keeping the borders straight and even. Add a hanging sleeve to the back of the design, or add hanging loops at regular intervals along the top.

a

b

c

d

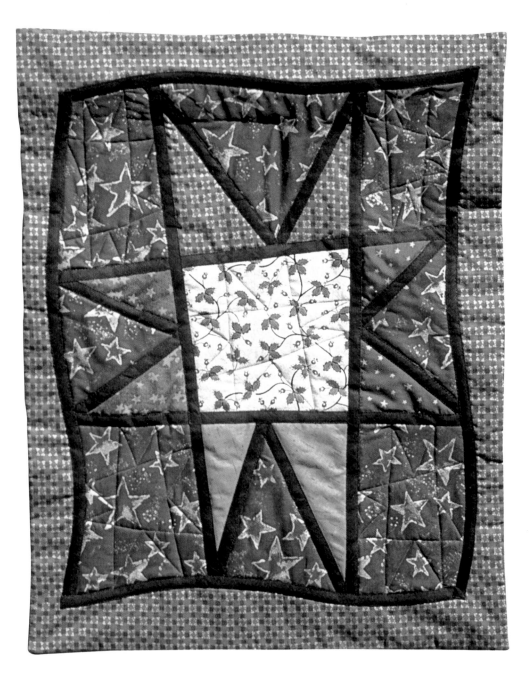

❂ THE CHRISTMAS STORY ❂

Crazy Christmas Star

Take all the tricky measuring out of star blocks; this crazy star design couldn't be simpler to stitch! A hanging like this one would make a lovely Christmas present – if you're confident, you could stitch two or three at the same time.

FINISHED SIZE: 26 x 22in (66 x 56cm)

EASINESS RATING: Very easy; a great starter project if you're new to stained glass patchwork. To make the design even easier, miss out the quilted star shapes at stages 6 and 7.

STITCHING TIP: *Remember that this is a crazy star, so the points are asymmetrical – remember to lay the templates right side up on the right side of the fabric.*

You will need

❊ two 25 x 21in (64 x 54cm) rectangles of green print fabric
❊ 22 x 18in (56 x 45cm) red Christmas print fabric
❊ 25 x 21in (64 x 54cm) compressed wadding
❊ 9in (23cm) square of cream Christmas print fabric for the centre of the star
❊ 8in (20cm) square of four different green Christmas print fabrics
❊ 7yd (7m) black bias binding, ½in (12mm) wide
❊ black, red and green sewing threads
❊ chalk marker
❊ extra fabric for a hanging sleeve, or ribbon or tape for display loops

Instructions

1 Trace or photocopy templates **A, B, C, D, E, F, G, H** and **I** from pages 73-75. Use template I to cut a patch from the cream fabric. Cut pieces A and B from one of the green print fabrics, C and D from another, E and F from the third, and G and H from the fourth.

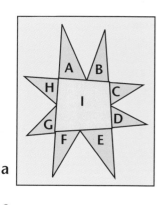

a

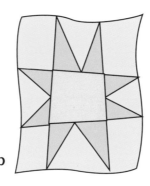

b

c

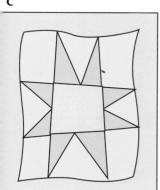

2 Lay the patches on the rectangle of red fabric and pin them in place to create a crazy star shape (**a**). Now cut the edges of the red rectangle into long S-shaped lines as shown (**b**); you don't have to be accurate about this, but if you're not sure about doing it 'cold', mark the lines with chalk first.

3 Lay the wadding on a flat surface and cover it with one of the green rectangles, right side up. Position the star design on top of the green fabric so that there is a roughly even border of fabric all the way around (**c**).

4 Add the lines of bias binding, following the sequence shown (**d**); you don't need to worry about neatening the ends of the binding at the tips of the points, as these will be covered by the final line of bias binding.

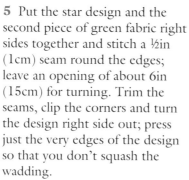

5 Put the star design and the second piece of green fabric right sides together and stitch a ½in (1cm) seam round the edges; leave an opening of about 6in (15cm) for turning. Trim the seams, clip the corners and turn the design right side out; press just the very edges of the design so that you don't squash the wadding.

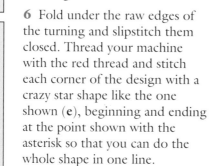

6 Fold under the raw edges of the turning and slipstitch them closed. Thread your machine with the red thread and stitch each corner of the design with a crazy star shape like the one shown (**e**), beginning and ending at the point shown with the asterisk so that you can do the whole shape in one line.

d

Again, you don't need to be accurate about this stitching – the whole charm of this design comes from its higgledy piggledy lines – but if you're not confident just launching in, draw a rough design out in chalk first.

7 Stitch a final star shape in the centre patch in the same way; make this one a bit larger.

e

8 Add hanging loops at even intervals along the top, or a hanging sleeve on the back, to complete the design.

✪ THE CHRISTMAS STORY ✪

Blue & Gold Star

A large golden star hangs in a shaded blue background, cleverly outlined by the unusual arrangement of straight lines; the inspiration for this design was an Oriental screen. The straight lines are offset in turn by a curvilinear star design in free machine quilting.

FINISHED SIZE: 40in (102cm) square

EASINESS RATING: Medium; this isn't a difficult design to stitch, but it is large, and you need to be confident with machining to quilt it with the continuous star design. If you'd like to try an easier version, stitch the design as a flat piece of appliqué, or quilt round each patch individually by hand or machine.

STITCHING TIP: *As all the stained glass patchwork lines in this design are straight, you don't need bias binding; try ribbon or seam tape instead. Seam binding in particular is often cheap – a great bonus when you need such a large amount.*

You will need

※ 41in (104cm) square of plain mid blue fabric for the backing and binding
※ 40in (102cm) square of compressed wadding
※ 8in (20cm) square of cream fabric for the centre of the star
※ 15 x 20in (40 x 50cm) gold and cream print fabric
※ 15 x 20in (40 x 50cm) pale yellow fabric
※ 15 x 20in (40 x 50cm) rich yellow fabric
※ large scraps of plain or small-print blue fabrics, shading from pale through to medium; you need five or six fat quarters in total
※ roughly 25yd (25m) royal blue tape, ½in (12mm) wide
※ royal blue sewing thread
※ yellow machine quilting thread
※ pack of dressmaker's tracing paper
※ soft pencil, ruler
※ extra fabric for a hanging sleeve, or ribbon or tape for display loops

Instructions

1 Trace or photocopy templates **A**, **B**, **C** and **D** from pages 76-77. Use template A to cut a single patch from the cream fabric. Use template B to cut five patches from the gold and cream print, template C to cut five patches from the pale yellow, and template D to cut five patches from the rich yellow; remember to lay the templates right side up on the right side of the fabric.

2 Following the layout shown (**a**), pin the patches in position in the centre of the wadding square to create a five-pointed star. (Look carefully at how the patches go together to make the star; it's not as obvious as it first seems!)

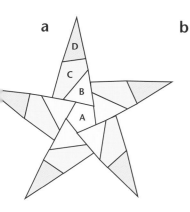

a

b

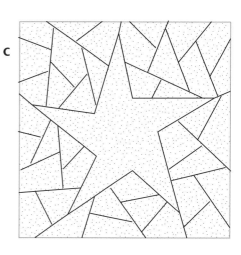

c

Cut a 40in (102cm) square of dressmaker's tracing paper; you may have to join two sheets to create a large enough square. Lay the square over the wadding, and trace the outlines of the star tape onto the paper (**b**). Now use a ruler and pencil to draw random straight lines to divide up each background section behind the star (**c**); exactly where you draw these lines isn't important, but have a look at the drawing and the main photograph to get the idea.

Beginning with the patches nearest the star, cut a few shapes at a time out of the tracing paper and use them as templates for cutting patches from the palest blue fabrics. *Don't* be tempted to cut all the templates out of the paper at once; I promise you you'll never remember which bit goes where! As you cut each patch, pin it in position on the wadding and throw away the template.

Continue working outwards in the same way, using increasingly dark patches of blue fabric, until all the patches have been cut out and pinned in position.

You now need to look carefully at your design to work out the T-junctions (see page 2); these will vary depending on exactly how you've divided up the patches. Stitch strips of ribbon or tape along the joins between patches, working your way through the sequence of T-junctions until all the pins are covered. (If you find that you've forgotten one T-junction, simply slit a few stitches and slip the end of the tape or ribbon underneath.)

Lay the blue backing fabric right side down on a flat surface and position the star design, right side up, on top, so that there's an even border of fabric all the way around. Secure the layers using your favourite method (tacking, safety pins, quilt glue, tack gun etc).

Thread your machine with the yellow machine quilting thread, drop the feed dogs, and fit the embroidery foot. Beginning in the centre of the design, work a pattern of swirly stars; you may find it helpful to practise this on a smaller piece first. If you work in a slow spiral around the work, you'll find that you can quilt the entire piece with

one line of stitching (honest!). The yellow stitching goes over the blue tape and acts as a good counterpoint to all the straight lines.

9 Once the quilting is complete, fold the edges of the backing square over to the front of the work and tack them in place; cover the raw edge with a final border of blue tape. Add hanging loops or a hanging sleeve to complete the design.

✪ **THE CHRISTMAS STORY** ✪

Church Window

You've probably seen the work of Dilys Fronks and Angela Besley at quilt shows; Dilys does wonderful scenes behind ornate cutaway gates, and Angela (my Mum!) does Rose Window patchwork, where she appliqués bright fabric patches onto dark backgrounds. This window design seems to have echoes of both their work, though I've created it in stained glass patchwork.

FINISHED SIZE: 22 x 39in (56 x 99cm)

EASINESS RATING: Challenging; there aren't many different fabrics in this design, but there are lots of little shaped patches to outline, so you'll need patience.

STITCHING TIP: *Using a multicoloured fabric is a great way of creating colour variations without extra piecing! I've used a random-dyed batik for the coloured sections of this design.*

You will need

❄ two 22 x 39in (56 x 99cm) rectangles of black fabric for the window border
❄ 18 x 35in (45 x 90cm) multicoloured fabric for the background, plus two 39 x 4in (99 x 10cm) strips and two 24 x 4in (61 x 10cm) strips of the same fabric for the bindings
❄ 22 x 39in (56 x 99cm) 2oz wadding
❄ 6in (15cm) square of pale yellow fabric for the centre of the star
❄ 9 x 6in (23 x 15cm) mid yellow fabric for the outside of the star
❄ extra fabric for a hanging sleeve or tape for hanging loops
❄ roughly 17yd (16m) of black bias binding, ¼in (6mm) wide
❄ black sewing thread
❄ pale crayon, black felt pen, ruler
❄ large piece of paper (a sheet of newspaper will do)

Instructions

1 Trace or photocopy the window design (**A**) on pages 78-79, and do a second tracing or photocopy as a mirror image. Fold the sheet of newspaper in half down its length; pin the designs to the top of the piece of newspaper, so that the dotted lines align with the fold, and draw parallel straight lines to extend the lines marked with arrows by 18in (45cm) (**a**). Draw in the bottom edges to create edges of the three window sections as shown (**b**). Go over the lines with black felt pen to make them stronger.

2 Fold one of the rectangles of black fabric in half down its

length and press, then unfold it and lay the fabric, right side up, over the drawing so that the fold aligns with the dotted centre line on the design; pin securely. A lightbox is useful for the next stage; if you haven't got one, tape the design to a window on a sunny day so that you can see the lines through the fabric. Use pale crayon to trace all the lines of the design onto the black fabric. Unpin, and press the fold out of the fabric.

3 Lay the multicoloured fabric right side up on a flat surface and cover it with the marked black fabric, right side up. Pin the layers together, then stitch round all the lines of the design with a small zigzag.

a

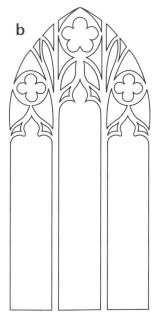
b

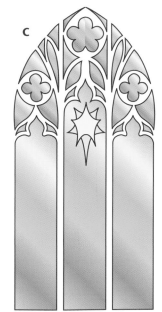
c

d

On the front of the design, carefully cut away the black fabric inside the stitching lines, as close to the zigzag as possible, to reveal the coloured fabric. (Be careful not to cut the coloured fabric as you do this.)

Trace or photocopy the star shapes (**B** and **C**) on page 80. Use shape B as a template to cut a patch from the darker yellow fabric, and C to cut one from the pale yellow. Lay the patches on top of each other near the top of the central window panel (**c**).

Using a pencil or crayon, draw random wiggly lines across the three main window sections and out from the star (**d**). These don't have to be exactly the same as mine, but the drawing shows the general idea.

Lay the wadding down on a flat surface and cover it with with the design, right side up. Secure the layers using your favourite method (tacking, safety pins, quilt glue, tack gun etc).

Look carefully at the design to see where the T-junctions (see page 2) are, and stitch bias binding onto the lines in sequence. Once all the lines are covered, outline each of the large window panels, and each of the smaller ones, with bias binding, over the zigzagged lines. The smaller apertures are a bit fiddly, so take them slowly!

Lay the second rectangle of black fabric, right side down, on a flat surface and cover it with the design, right side up. Pin the layers together, then stitch a line of quilting, by hand or machine, about ¼in (6mm) outside the arched shape of the window.

10 Use the long strips of multicoloured fabric to bind the sides of the panel, then bind the top and bottom edges with the shorter strips. Add a hanging sleeve or display loops.

✪ THE CHRISTMAS STORY ✪

Angel

Christmas wouldn't be Christmas without an angel singing out the good news – this rather elegant one is made more ethereal by the outlines of gold bias binding. I found a wonderful random batik print in bright colours for the outer fabric, but you might prefer a plainer one.

FINISHED SIZE: 29in (74cm) square

EASINESS RATING: Best for stitchers **confident** with stained glass patchwork; there aren't many fabric patches, but some of them are quite small, and there are lots of lines of bias binding.

STITCHING TIP: *If you want to add extra quilting to your angel design, the large areas of border fabric would lend themselves to quilting by hand or machine.*

You will need

❋ 29in (74cm) square of brightly patterned fabric for the border
❋ 29in (74cm) square of 2oz wadding
❋ 32in (81cm) square of dark pink fabric for the backing and binding
❋ 22in (56cm) square of pale yellow fabric for the background
❋ 6in (15cm) square of mid yellow fabric for the halo
❋ 12in (30cm) square of white fabric for the wings
❋ 10in (25cm) squares of pale aqua mottled fabric for the upper dress, and mid aqua mottled fabric for the skirt and dress details
❋ 7in (18cm) square of dark brown fabric for the hair
❋ 12 x 4in (30 x 10cm) pale patterned brown fabric for the lute
❋ scrap of mid brown fabric for the lute back
❋ scraps of flesh-coloured fabric for the hands and face
❋ 12yd (12m) gold bias binding, ¼in (6mm) wide
❋ 18in (50cm) gold flower braid for the skirt and headdress
❋ cream sewing thread
❋ soft pencil, large sheet of paper, ruler
❋ extra fabric for a hanging sleeve, or ribbon or tape for display loop

Instructions

Draw a 20in (50cm) square on your paper; divide this into a grid of five squares by five, each square measuring 4in or 10cm. Use the grid method to enlarge the design on page 31; copy the lines of the design onto your grid, enlarging them as you go, to create a full-size pattern.

Lay your pale yellow fabric over the design and trace all the solid lines in pencil. Cut the paper pattern up along the solid lines, discard the background pieces, and use the other shapes as templates to cut patches from the appropriate fabrics, laying the templates right side up on the right side of the fabric.

Lay the wing shapes over the paper pattern and trace the dotted lines to create the feather designs. Do the same with the lines on the dress pieces, or draw them in by eye; draw in the rays around the halo, too.

Lay the marked yellow fabric on a flat surface and position the patches on top to create the design; pin, then go round the edges with a small zigzag to hold the patches in place.

Begin to add the lines of bias binding, looking carefully at the lines of the design so that you add the T-junctions in order. Do all the lines except the quatrefoil outline. Now stitch a short piece of the gold braid round the angel's head as a headdress, and add lengths down her skirt as shown on the drawing.

Press the design well from the back. Lay the coloured border fabric out on a flat surface, right side up, and position the angel design on top so that there's an equal margin round each part of the quatrefoil (**a**). Stitch a small zigzag round the quatrefoil shape.

On the front of the work, cut away excess yellow fabric just **outside** the line of zigzag to reveal the shaped border (**b**). On the back of the work, cut away the unwanted border fabric by cutting just **inside** the line of zigzag.

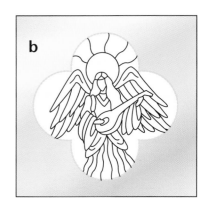

8 Lay the pink backing fabric on a flat surface, right side down, and position the wadding on top so that there's an even border of fabric all the way around. Lay the angel design on top of the wadding, right side up; pin the layers together. Now add a line of gold bias binding round the quatrefoil shape.

9 Fold the pink fabric over to the front of the work in a single fold, mitring the corners, and pin or tack it in place. Work a wiggly line of small zigzag around this border as shown (**c**), stitching 1-1½in (2-3.5cm) in from the folded edge. Trim the excess pink fabric away just beyond the stitching to create a wiggly border (**d**).

10 Cover the zigzag stitching with a final line of gold bias binding, then add a hanging sleeve to the back of the panel or display loops along the top.

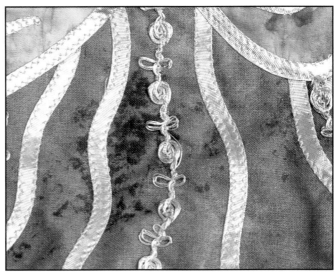

✪ THE CHRISTMAS STORY ✪

Bethlehem Scene

O little town of Bethlehem, how still we see thee lie …
A clear blue sky shines above the simple buildings of
the city, created in different metallic fabrics to catch
the light.

FINISHED SIZE: 13 x 31in (33 x 79cm)

EASINESS RATING: Easy to medium; the patches are large and the design is easy to assemble.

STITCHING TIP: *If you're wary of working with metallics, see the notes on page 8 – or create the scene in Christmassy cotton prints instead.*

You will need

❋ 15 x 33in (37 x 83cm) black fabric for the backing and binding
❋ 7 x 31in (18 x 79cm) plain blue fabric for the sky
❋ 13 x 31in (33 x 79cm) compressed wadding
❋ large scraps of metallic fabrics in different colours and patterns; the largest piece needed (for the castle shape) is 12in (30cm) square
❋ 10yd (10m) black bias binding, ½in (12mm) wide
❋ black sewing thread
❋ soft pencil
❋ extra fabric for a hanging sleeve, or ribbon or tape for display loops

Instructions

1 Trace or photocopy the two halves of the Bethlehem scene from pages 82-85. Cut the drawing up to make templates, and use these to cut patches from the metallic fabrics, laying the templates right side up on the right sides of the fabric.

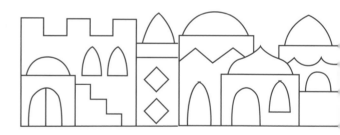

2 Lay the wadding on a flat surface and position the strip of blue fabric along the top of the wadding, raw edges matching. Lay the other patches in position, overlapping the sky piece when necessary, to create the Bethlehem scene; pin in place.

3 Following the sequence shown opposite, stitch on the lines of bias binding in order.

4 Lay the black fabric right side down on a flat surface and position the design, right side up, on top so that there is an even border of fabric all the way around. Fold the raw edges to the front of the work in a double fold; stitch down the fold by hand or machine.

5 Add a hanging sleeve on the back, or display loops of tape or ribbon at equal intervals along the top edge.

✪ THE CHRISTMAS STORY ✪

Crib Triptych

A crib scene is a traditional centrepiece for Christmas decorations – why not stitch your own triptych, showing the wise men and shepherds visiting the stable in Bethlehem. This design uses what I call 'stained glass stitchery'; it's done in the same basic way as stained glass patchwork, but uses lines of black machine satin stitch between the patches instead of bias binding.

FINISHED SIZE: Each individual panel is 13 x 19in (33 x 48cm)
The complete triptych measures 39 x 19in (99 x 48cm)

EASINESS RATING: For the confident stitcher only; each design has lots of lines of stitching. If you fancy trying the technique, do a single panel to see how you get on.

STITCHING TIP: *Use a firm fabric for the foundation; unwashed heavy calico is ideal. This, along with the tear-away foundation paper, will help to keep your stitching lines smooth.*

You will need

for each panel:
* ❋ 11 x 18in (28 x 45cm) firm cream or white fabric for the foundation
* ❋ 11 x 18in (28 x 45cm) Stitch 'n' Tear or similar tear-away foundation paper
* ❋ 8in (20cm) square of navy and gold starry sky print
* ❋ large scraps of mid green and dark green cotton fabric for the trees
* ❋ large scrap of mottled brown fabric for the paving

* ❋ small scraps of flesh-coloured fabric for the hands and faces
* ❋ assorted large scraps of other fabrics in appropriate colours for the clothing, sheep, haloes, beards etc; I've used exotic prints and metallics for the wise men, homely stripes and prints for the shepherds and Joseph, traditional blues for Mary, and white for the swaddling clothes and the sheep
* ❋ large reel of black machine embroidery thread
* ❋ 1½yd (1.5m) black bias binding, ½in (12mm) wide
* ❋ soft pencil, chalk marker

to make up the triptych:
* ❋ two 40 x 20in (102 x 50cm) rectangles of contrast fabric for the border
* ❋ three 13 x 19in (33 x 48cm) rectangles of thick card
* ❋ blue sewing thread

Instructions

each panel is made in the same way:

1 Trace or photocopy the appropriate design from pages 86-88, enlarging from A4 to A3. Lay the white or cream fabric over the design and trace all the solid lines in pencil.

2 Cut up the design along the solid lines and use the pieces as templates to cut patches from the appropriate fabrics, remembering to lay the templates right side up on the right side of the fabric. As you cut each fabric patch, add about ⅛in (1-2mm) extra all round the edge, just to give you a small overlap when you lay the pieces down.

3 Pin the patches in position on the foundation fabric, and stitch round the outlines with a small zigzag to secure the patches.

4 In pencil, draw extra lines on the patches to correspond to the dotted lines on the design; these don't need to be too exact. You're now ready for the stained glass stitchery.

5 Thread your machine with the black embroidery thread and set it to the stitch length for satin stitch. (If your machine doesn't have a specific satin stitch, set it to the smallest practical zigzag length – try a sample out on some scrap fabric.) Set the width to about 3.5. Slip the sheet of tear-away foundation paper under the design and pin in position. Look carefully at the design to work out the T-junctions (for instance, see diagram **a** for the first lines to be stitched on the wise men panel), and stitch these in sequence with lines of satin stitch. Leave the outside arched frame shape unstitched.

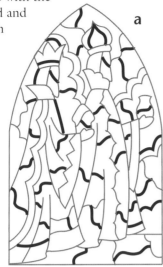

6 Tear all the foundation paper away from the back of the design, and press it from the back with a steam iron. If the stitching has distorted the fabric at all, spray the whole design thoroughly from a water bottle, then pin it out flat and allow it to dry overnight.

7 If you're doing just one panel, cut a 14 x 20in (36 x 51cm) rectangle of border fabric. Lay the design on top, and stitch a small zigzag round the arched outside shape; cut away excess fabric from outside the stitching line on the front of the work to reveal the border. Add a line of bias binding round the edges of the arched shape to complete the design. The individual panel can now be finished off in any way you choose – you can quilt it, or leave it as a piece of plain appliqué. If you want to build it into the triptych, follow the instructions below.

To make the triptych:

1 Stitch all three panels up to stage 6 as described above. Lay one of the large rectangles of border fabric on a flat surface, right side up, and position the three designs in order; leave roughly 4in (10cm) between the panels, and a border of about 2in (5cm) all round the edges (**b**).

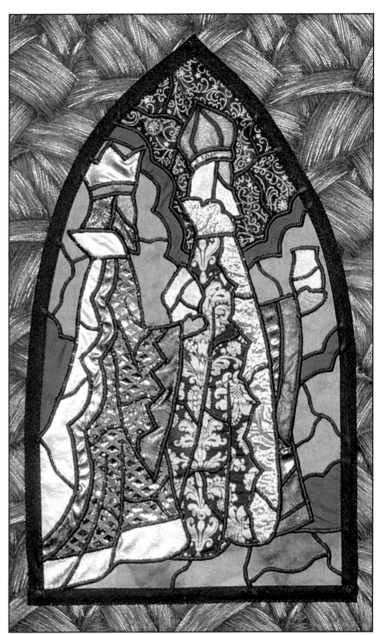

Pin the panels in position, then stitch them to the border fabric as described in step 7 above. You now have the front of the triptych.

2 Put the two rectangles of border and backing fabric right sides together and pin. Stitch a ½in (1cm) seam up the sides and along the top; don't stitch the bottom edge. Trim the seams, clip the corners and turn to the right side; press the seams at the edges of the work.

3 The rectangle should now measure 39in (99cm) wide. Measure in 13in (33cm) from each edge and draw a chalk line to divide the panel into three. Thread your machine with blue thread and stitch a line of straight stitching down each chalk line (**c**); finish the line 1in (2.5cm) short of the open edge.

4 You've now created three pockets. Slip a piece of card into each pocket; press the raw edges of the fabric under, and slipstitch the opening closed. Your triptych is now ready to stand on a shelf or table – put a few miniature sheep in front if you have any!

✪ LOOKS LIKE SNOW ... ✪

Snow-Scene Stocking

Make sure that Father Christmas has got somewhere to put all those goodies when he comes down the chimney – hang up a stocking, complete with reindeer in the snow, to make him feel at home while he eats the mince pies and knocks back the sherry!

FINISHED SIZE: The stocking is 22in (65cm) tall

EASINESS RATING: Fairly simple; the stained glass patchwork design is small and relatively straightforward, and the stocking is easy to make up.

STITCHING TIP: *If the stocking's going to be used by small children, it's probably safest to leave off the beads.*

You will need

❋ two 22 x 15in (56 x 38cm) rectangles of snowy Christmas print fabric
❋ two 24 x 15in (61 x 38cm) rectangles of green or other toning fabric to line the stocking
❋ two 24 x 15in (61 x 38cm) rectangles of compressed wadding
❋ 14 x 6in (36 x 15cm) white cotton fabric or felt for the snow
❋ 6in (15cm) square of mottled pale brown fabric for the reindeer
❋ 2 x 3in (5 x 8cm) mottled mid brown fabric
❋ 9 x 6in (23 x 15cm) pale green fabric for the tree outside
❋ 7 x 4in (18 x 10cm) mid green fabric for the tree inside
❋ 4yd (4m) red-brown bias binding, ¼in (6mm) wide
❋ 2yd (2m) red-brown bias binding, 1in (2.5cm) wide
❋ red-brown, brown and white sewing threads
❋ soft pencil, black felt pen, large sheet of newspaper or cartridge paper
❋ white pearly beads in assorted sizes
❋ small brown bead for the reindeer's eye

Instructions

1 Cut a rectangle of paper 22 x 15in (56 x 38cm) and draw a simple stocking shape onto the paper as shown (**a**). Once you're happy with the shape, cut it out; draw a second line 2in (5cm) down from the top (**b**).

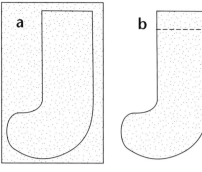

2 Put the two rectangles of green lining fabric right sides together and use the stocking template to cut two shapes, mirror images. Cut two stocking shapes from the wadding.

3 Cut the top off the stocking template, along the dotted line, and use this new, shorter stocking design to cut two shapes from the print fabric – mirror images again.

4 Trace or photocopy the reindeer design on page 89; go over the lines with black felt pen to make them stronger. Lay one of the print stockings (the one with the foot pointing to the left) over the design, right side up, and trace the lines of the design onto the print fabric (**c**); you may need the help of a lightbox or a sunny window to do this. Extend the wiggly snow line to the edges of the print fabric.

5 Cut out the reindeer and tree shapes along the solid lines and use the pieces as templates to cut patches from the relevant materials; then cut out the central patch from the reindeer, as marked by the dotted lines, and use this patch as a template to cut a shape from the mid brown fabric.

6 Lay the patches in position over the drawing on the print fabric and pin them in place (**d**); secure them with a line of small zigzag. Position the white fabric, right side up, behind the print fabric (**e**), and stitch through the two layers along the wiggly snow line. Trim the white fabric to the shape of the stocking (**f**). On the front of the work, cut away the excess print fabric below the stitch line to reveal the snow (**g**).

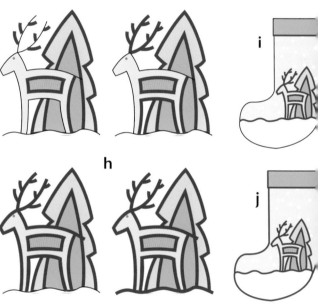

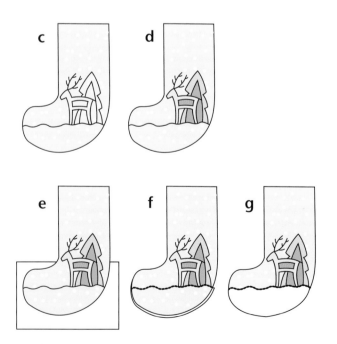

7 Create two 'sandwiches' with a layer of print fabric (right side out), a layer of wadding, and a layer of green lining fabric (right side out). These will create the two sides of the stocking.

8 Add the lines of bias binding in order, following the sequence shown (**h**), and stitching by hand or machine. On each 'sandwich', fold the wadding and green fabric over to the right side and stitch in place; cover the line of stitching with a line of the narrow bias binding, to create a cuff at the top of the stocking (**i**).

9 Put the two sides of the stocking together, right sides out, and pin; bind the raw edges with the wider bias binding, using the same line of binding to make a loop at the right-hand edge of the stocking top (**j**).

10 Using white thread, stitch pearl beads onto the 'sky' and 'snow' at irregular intervals; using brown thread, stitch on the reindeer's eye. Then hang up the stocking and put out the mince pies …

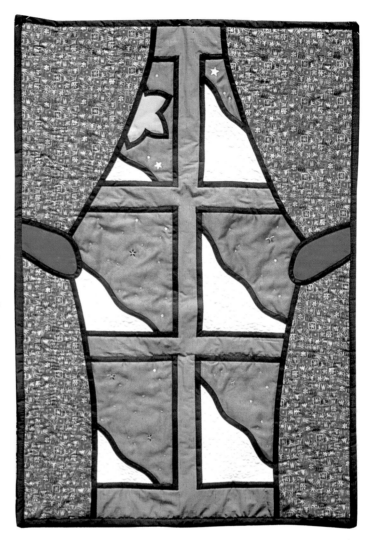

✪ **LOOKS LIKE SNOW ...** ✪

Starry Night

A golden star peeps in through the curtains on a snowy night – better to be indoors than out! I've echoed the large star with smaller star sequins in the sky; you could achieve a similar effect with a gold and blue star-print fabric.

FINISHED SIZE: 28 x 40in (71 x 102cm)

EASINESS RATING: Medium; the patches are large and the binding is quite wide, so it's not a difficult design, but there are quite a few pieces. To make it easier, omit the free machine quilting on the snow patches and the hand quilting on the curtains.

STITCHING TIP: *This is a good project to try out a bit of vermicelli stitching. Don't worry if the pattern you make isn't very smooth; you're just putting a bit of texture onto the snow sections.*

You will need

- 32 x 44in (81 x 112cm) black fabric for the backing and binding
- 28 x 40in (71 x 102cm) green fabric for the background – plain, or with a small print
- 28 x 40in (71 x 102cm) 2oz wadding
- six 10in (25cm) squares of blue fabric for the sky
- 10 x 30in (25 x 75cm) plain white fabric for the snow
- two 12 x 40in (30 x 102cm) rectangles of Christmas print fabric for the curtains
- two 7 x 5in (18 x 13cm) rectangles of toning fabric for the tie-backs
- 7in (18cm) square of golden yellow fabric for the star
- 10yd (10m) of black bias binding, roughly ½in (12mm) wide
- black, white and golden yellow sewing threads
- quilting threads to match the curtain fabric
- gold star sequins in assorted sizes
- soft pencil

Instructions

1 Trace or photocopy the snow shape (**A**) on page 90, and use this to cut six 'snow' patches from the white fabric (remember to lay the template right side up on the right side of the fabric). Pin one snow patch to the bottom of each blue sky square.

2 Trace or photocopy the star shape (**B**) on page 90, and use it as a template to cut one shape from the yellow fabric; pin this into the sky on one of the blue squares.

3 Put the two rectangles of 'curtain' fabric right sides together and cut down one long edge (**a**) roughly in the shape shown (you don't need to be too exact as long as the curtains are symmetrical).

4 Trace or photocopy the tie-back shape (**C**) from page 90; put the two rectangles of tie-back fabric right sides together, and use the shape to cut two mirror-image patches.

5 Lay the rectangle of green fabric on a flat surface, right side up, and position the sky squares on top at equal intervals – roughly 2in (5cm) apart and 3in (8cm) in from the edges. Make sure that the square with the star on it is at the top left (**b**). Pin the curtain and tie-back shapes on top (**c**); adjust the position of any of the pieces if necessary to make a more pleasing composition. Once you're happy, stitch a small zigzag down the inner edge of the curtain sections and round the visible parts of each square to secure the patches to the green fabric. On the back of the work, cut away any excess fabric from behind the curtain shapes.

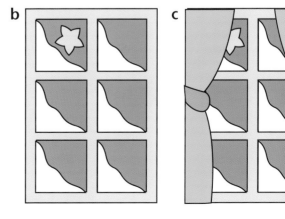

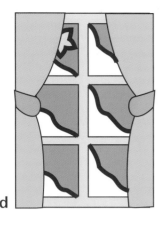   

d

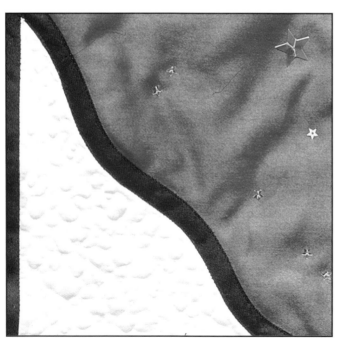

6 Lay the wadding out on a flat surface and position the design, right side up, on top. Secure the layers using your preferred method (tacking, safety pins, quilt glue, tack gun).

7 Thread your machine with white thread, drop the feed dogs, and put on the embroidery foot. Beginning near one edge, work a large free 'vermicelli' stitch across each white snow section. Move the fabric smoothly and evenly under the embroidery foot; if you're new to this type of quilting, practise on a small spare 'sandwich' of fabric and wadding first. Don't try and follow a specific pattern; the charm of this kind of quilting comes from its random effect.

8 Follow the sequence shown (**d**) to add the lines of bias binding, stitching by hand or machine; keep the corners of the squares sharp and crisp.

9 Lay the backing fabric, right side down, on a flat surface and position the design, right side up, on top so that there's an even border of black fabric all round the edges. Make the border the same width as the lines of bias binding, or just slightly wider. Fold the raw edges to the front in a double fold, mitring the corners neatly, and stitch the folded edge down by hand or machine (**e**) to create a frame around the scene.

10 Using the quilting thread, stitch some random lines of hand quilting down the curtain sections to look like folds. Using yellow thread, stitch a scattering of star sequins onto each sky section (**f**). Add a hanging sleeve to the back, or hanging loops at even intervals along the top edge, to complete your panel.

e   f

✪ LOOKS LIKE SNOW ... ✪

Midnight Skies

Midnight on Christmas Eve, and all is calm as we peep through to the night sky. The backgrounds for these two snowy scenes are created in the same way; the difference comes from the stained glass patchwork done on top of them. For one I've used lines of black tape to create a view through a casement window; the other is glimpsed through a screen of silver snowflakes.

FINISHED SIZE: Each scene is 17 x 27in (43 x 69cm)

EASINESS RATING: Medium for the casement window; **quite a lot more challenging** for the snowflakes, as there are plenty of fiddly curves which require patience.

STITCHING TIP: *As all the lines within the casement window are straight, you can use ribbon or seam binding for these lines – often a lot cheaper than bias binding. If you're worried about the background fabrics fraying, you can back them with light iron-on Vilene to stabilise them.*

You will need

for the casement window:

❋ 18 x 5in (45 x 13cm) rectangles of eight different snowy sky fabrics, ranging from pale to dark; I've used a series of blue and silver cotton prints

❋ 18 x 28in (45 x 71cm) thin white foundation fabric, eg lawn or fine calico

❋ 18 x 28in (45 x 71cm) compressed wadding

❋ two 18 x 28in (45 x 71cm) rectangles of plain mid blue fabric for the border and the backing

❋ 11yd (11m) black bias binding, ¼in (6mm) wide

❋ silver, blue, white and black sewing threads

❋ soft pencil, black felt pen

❋ large sheet of white paper

❋ white or opalescent snowflake sequins

❋ extra fabric for a hanging sleeve, or tape for display loops

for the snowflake scene:

❋ sky fabrics and foundation fabric as described above

❋ 18 x 28in (45 x 71cm) compressed wadding

❋ 18 x 28in (45 x 71cm) bonded silver fabric

- ❄ 19 x 29in (49 x 74cm) plain mid blue fabric for the backing and binding
- ❄ 15yd (15m) silver bias binding, ¼in (6mm) wide (the fusible binding is perfect)
- ❄ silver and white sewing threads
- ❄ soft pencil
- ❄ several sheets of white paper
- ❄ extra fabric for a hanging sleeve, or tape for display loops

Instructions

to make the casement window:

1 Cut one long edge of each sky strip into a random wiggly line. Lay the white foundation fabric on a flat surface and position the strips of fabric on top, shading them from light down to dark, and overlapping them so that the wiggly lines are on top (**a**). Set your sewing machine to fairly large zigzag and thread it with silver thread; work a line of stitching along each wiggly edge to create the background for the scene.

2 Cut a rectangle of paper the same size as the wadding and draw a border 1½in (4cm) in from each edge. Draw a curved design so that the top of the central curve touches the drawn border; you now have a decorative window shape (**b**). Cover the inside of this shape with regular repeats of design **A** on page 91, as shown (**c**); go over the lines with black felt pen to make them stronger. Lay the background design, right side up, over the drawing and pin securely in place; trace the lines with soft pencil – you may need the help of a lightbox or a sunny window for this stage.

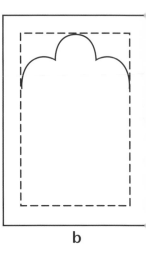

a   **b**

3 Lay one of the rectangles of plain blue fabric right side up on a flat surface and position the marked design, right side up, on top; pin the layers together. Work a line of small zigzag round the edge of the window shape. On the front of the work, trim away the excess background just outside the stitching line to reveal the border (**d**). (If you wish, you can cut away the excess blue fabric from inside the stitching line on the back of the work.)

4 Lay the wadding on a flat surface and position the marked background, right side up, on top; pin securely or tack. Add lines of bias binding or tape over all the straight lines inside the window shape; do some of the short lines of the pattern first as shown (**e**), and you'll then be able to add long lines across the shape (**f**). Don't add binding round the outline at this stage.

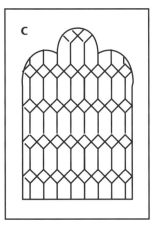

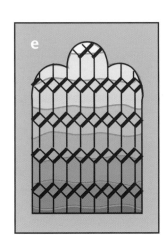

Put the design and the second rectangle of blue fabric right sides together and pin; stitch a ½in (12mm) seam round the edges, leaving a gap of about 8in (20cm) along the bottom edge for turning. Trim the seams, clip the corners and turn the work to the right side; press just the very edges of the seams, so that you don't squash the padding.

Turn in the seam allowances on the opening, and slipstitch it closed. Add a line of bias binding round the edge of the window shape to secure the two layers together.

Using white thread, stitch snowflake sequins randomly across the window section of the design; add a hanging sleeve or display loops to complete the panel.

• make the snowflake scene:
Create the background as described in step 1 on page 44. Trace or photocopy the two different snowflake designs (**A** and **B**) on page 92, then cut several of each from folded paper to create whole snowflakes.

a   b

On the back of the bonded silver fabric, lay out several whole and half snowflakes to create the pattern shown (**a**), making sure that the tips join. Trace the lattice shape you've created onto the fabric, then cut out the shape (**b**). Lay this lattice onto the background you've created (**c**) and pin in position (if the silver fabric you've chosen shows pin marks, pin just at the very edges of the fabric where the holes will be covered by the binding).

3 Use the tip of the iron to fuse bias binding all round the edges of the snowflakes; you'll find that you can keep going in a continuous line all round the shaped tips of the snowflakes, simply crossing over the joined tips of the flakes as you come to them. Do the fusing slowly and carefully so that you keep the curves even and the points and corners sharp; it's a bit fiddly, but worth taking the time to do well.

c

4 Once all the binding is fused in place, lay the design right side up on the wadding, and stitch the binding in position by hand or machine.

5 Lay the rectangle of plain fabric right side down on a flat surface and position the design on top. Fold the raw edges to the front of the work in a single fold to create a neat border; secure the raw edges with a small line of zigzag. Cover the zigzag with a final border of bias binding. Add a hanging sleeve or display loops to complete the panel.

Baby's First Christmas

Welcome a new baby to his or her first Christmas with any of these four folksy designs. You can work them on ready-made bibs or towels for extra speed, or you could stitch several onto a little pram quilt or comforter.

FINISHED SIZE: Each design is around 6in (15cm) high and 4-5in (10-12cm) wide

EASINESS RATING: Very easy – the simplest designs in the book, perfect for an absolute beginner.

STITCHING TIP: *Towelling creates a slightly bumpy surface to work on; you'll find it easier if you secure the fabric patches in place with a line of small zigzag before you start adding the bias binding.*

You will need

for the star:
❋ white or cream towelling bib
❋ 5in (13cm) square of Christmas print fabric
❋ 1¼yd (1.2m) blue bias binding, ¼in (6mm) wide
❋ blue sewing thread
❋ soft pencil or chalk marker

for the heart:
❋ white or cream towelling bib
❋ 5in (13cm) square of Christmas print fabric
❋ 1¼yd (1.2m) blue bias binding, ¼in (6mm) wide
❋ blue sewing thread
❋ soft pencil or chalk marker

for the Christmas tree:
❋ small pale green towel
❋ 5in (13cm) square of green Christmas print fabric for the tree
❋ scrap of red Christmas print fabric for the pot
❋ 1¼yd (1.2m) green bias binding, ¼in (6mm) wide
❋ green sewing thread
❋ soft pencil or chalk marker

for the stocking:
❋ small pale green towel
❋ 4in (10cm) square of red Christmas print fabric
❋ 4in (10cm) square of contrasting Christmas print fabric
❋ 1¼yd (1.2m) green bias binding, ¼in (6mm) wide
❋ green sewing thread
❋ soft pencil or chalk marker

Instructions

to make the star:

1 Trace or photocopy the star design (**A**) on page 93. Cut out the star shape along the solid line (don't worry about cutting off the ends of the dotted lines) and use it as a template to cut your fabric patch, remembering to place it right side up on the right side of your fabric.

2 Mark the positions of the dotted lines on your fabric patch in pencil or chalk (these don't have to be exact), then pin the patch to the centre of the bib front. Work a line of small machine zigzag around the patch to hold it in place on the towelling.

3 Add a line of bias binding all the way round the star, beginning and ending at one of the points; stitch the binding on by hand or machine.

4 On each pencil or chalk mark, add a short, straight line of binding so that it straddles the outline of the star; tuck the raw ends under neatly.

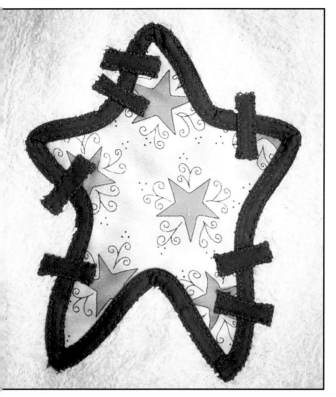

4 On each pencil or chalk mark, add a short, straight line of binding so that it straddles the outline of the tree; tuck the raw ends under neatly.

to make the stocking:

1 Trace or photocopy the stocking design (**D**) on page 93. Cut out the three pieces along the solid lines (don't worry about cutting off the ends of the dotted lines) and use these as templates to cut your fabric patches, remembering to place them right side up on the right side of your fabric.

2 Mark the positions of the dotted lines on your fabric patches in pencil or chalk (these don't have to be exact), then pin the patches near one corner of the towel front. Work a line of small machine zigzag around the patches to hold them in place on the towelling.

3 Add a line of bias binding across the join between the toe and the main stocking, stitching the binding on by hand or machine. Next, add a line around the main part of the stocking. Finally, make a complete line around the stocking top, tucking the raw ends under.

4 On each pencil or chalk mark, add a short, straight line of binding so that it straddles the outline of the stocking; tuck the raw ends under neatly.

) make the heart:

Trace or photocopy the heart design (**B**) on page 93. Cut out the heart shape along the solid line (don't worry about cutting off the ends of the dotted lines) and use it as a template to cut your fabric patch, remembering to place it right side up on the right side of your fabric.

Mark the positions of the dotted lines on your fabric patch in pencil or chalk (these don't have to be exact), then pin the patch to the centre of the bib front. Work a line of small machine zigzag around the patch to hold it in place on the towelling.

Add a line of bias binding all the way round the heart, beginning and ending at the tip; stitch the binding on by hand or machine.

On each pencil or chalk mark, add a short, straight line of binding so that it straddles the outline of the heart; tuck the raw ends under neatly.

) make the tree:

Trace or photocopy the tree design (**C**) on page 93. Cut out the two pieces along the solid lines (don't worry about cutting off the ends of the dotted lines) and use these as templates to cut your fabric patches, remembering to place them right side up on the right side of your fabric.

Mark the positions of the dotted lines on your fabric patches in pencil or chalk (these don't have to be exact), then pin the patches near one corner of the towel front. Work a line of small machine zigzag around the patches to hold them in place on the towelling.

Add a line of bias binding round the sides and bottom of the pot, stitching the binding on by hand or machine. Now add a single line all around the tree shape, beginning and ending at the top.

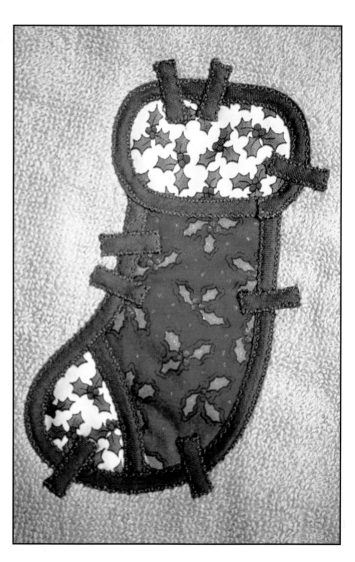

✪ CHRISTMAS IS COMING ✪

Christmas Keepsake Album

Memories are made of … Christmas pudding! Stitch an old-fashioned plum pudding to decorate a plain photograph album, and use it for all your Christmas keepsakes; how about photographs of the spread and everyone invited, plus a menu, and comments from all the guests?

FINISHED SIZE: The design is 7in (18cm) square

EASINESS RATING: Easy to medium; this is a small, relatively quick design with no extra quilting or embellishment, suitable for the confident beginner or those with a little experience of stained glass patchwork.

STITCHING TIP: *Adding the glue to the album rather than to the back of the design means that it's much less likely to seep through the fabric. If you find that the cream fabric is a bit translucent when you lay it on the album cover, back the design with a square of iron-on interfacing before you glue it to the album.*

You will need

❋ 7in (18cm) square of red Christmas print fabric for the border
❋ 6in (15cm) square of cream Christmas print fabric for the background
❋ 5in (13cm) square of mottled brown fabric for the pudding
❋ 5 x 3in (13 x 8cm) white plain or patterned fabric for the icing
❋ 6 x 3in (15 x 8cm) green Christmas print fabric for the plate
❋ scraps of plain or mottled green fabric for the holly leaves
❋ 3yd (3m) black bias binding, ¼in (6mm) wide
❋ black sewing thread
❋ soft pencil, black felt pen
❋ clear glue
❋ red photograph album at least 9in (23cm) wide

Instructions

Trace or photocopy the pudding design on page 94; go over the lines with black felt pen to make them stronger. Lay the cream background fabric over the design and trace the lines of the design in pencil, then cut up the paper pattern along the solid lines. Discard the background sections, and use the other pieces as templates to cut your fabric patches, remembering to place them right side up on the right side of your fabric.

Lay the patches in position over the drawing on the cream fabric and pin them in place (if you want, secure them with a line of small zigzag before you begin adding the binding).

Add the lines of bias binding in order, following the sequence shown below, and stitching by hand or machine.

When all the binding is in place, press the work thoroughly from the back; carefully trim away any stray threads from the border fabric if they are poking out beyond the final line of binding. Lay the design on the front of the photograph album; when you're happy with the positioning, draw round the edges of the square lightly with pencil, or by drawing the tip of a pin very gently round the edge. Remove the design, spread quite a thick layer of clear glue inside the marked square on the album cover, and leave the glue until it is nearly dry but still tacky; then position the design in place, cover with a heavy book, and leave overnight to dry.

Noel

Four bold letters spell out a Christmas greeting. I fell in love with the wonderful Florentine-style print I've used on each letter the moment I saw it in my local quilt shop; here it's set off by toning Christmas prints in different royal colours.

FINISHED SIZE: 12 x 48in (30 x 120cm)

EASINESS RATING: Quite straightforward; the letters are large and easy to work on. If you're quite new to stained glass patchwork, try leaving out the cornerpieces to make the panels simpler to create.

STITCHING TIP: *You don't have to join the panels the way I have; you could stitch them into a horizontal line instead, or even into a square.*

You will need

❋ 12in (30cm) square of exotic patterned fabric
❋ 12in (30cm) square of red Christmas print fabric
❋ 12in (30cm) square of blue Christmas print fabric
❋ four 12in (30cm) squares of green print or plain fabric
❋ four 12in (30cm) squares of compressed wadding
❋ two 13in (32cm) squares of red fabric (plain or small print)
❋ two 13in (32cm) squares of blue fabric (plain or small print)
❋ 6 x 12in (15 x 30cm) white-based Christmas print fabric
❋ 14yd (14m) black bias binding, ¼in (6mm) wide
❋ black and red sewing threads
❋ extra fabric for a hanging sleeve, or ribbon or tape for display loops

Instructions

1 Trace or photocopy the four letter templates and the corner template from pages 95-98; cut these up, and use them as templates to cut your fabric patches. Cut the left-hand shape of each letter from the exotic print; use the red print for the rest of the N and E, and the blue print for the rest of the O and the L. Cut 16 corner pieces from the white-based print.

2 Lay the four squares of wadding on a flat surface, and cover them with the squares of green fabric, right side up. Pin four corner pieces onto each square (**a**), then position the letter patches in position, one letter on each green square (**b**).

3 Stitch bias binding round the cornerpieces and down the wiggly centre line of each letter (**c**), then add the outlines to complete each letter (**d**).

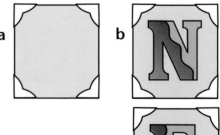

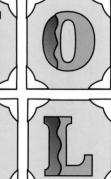

c   d

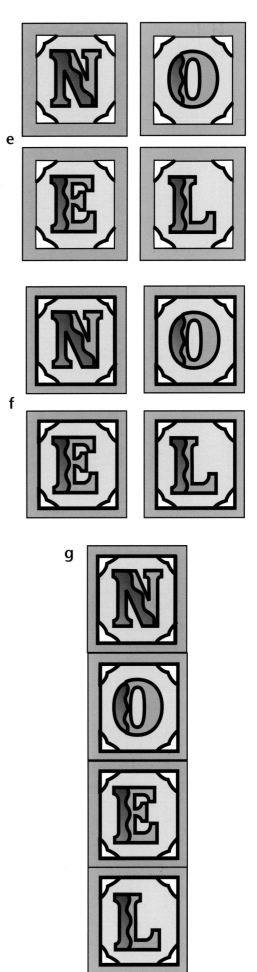

e

f

g

4 Lay the four squares of backing fabric (two red and two blue) on a flat surface, right sides down, and position the letter squares on top, right side up, so that there's an even border of fabric all the way around (**e**). Put the N and E on the blue squares, and the O and L on the red squares.

5 Fold the raw edges of fabric over to the front of each panel and secure with a line of tacking or small zigzag; cover the raw edges with a line of bias binding (**f**), keeping the lines straight and even.

6 Lay the letters out in order (to ensure that you join the correct edges!), then, two squares at a time, place them right sides together and oversew them along the folded edges. Once they're all joined (**g**), add a hanging sleeve to the back of the panel or display loops along the top.

✪ CHRISTMAS IS COMING ✪

Advent Calendar

Make the most of the Christmas countdown with a stained glass patchwork advent calendar; each little pocket holds a scrumptious treat. If you think your kids will have enough sweeties in their Christmas stockings, fill the pockets with tiny toys or little notes promising something special – for instance, 'You can help me ice the cake today'.

FINISHED SIZE: 35 x 30in (90 x 76cm)

EASINESS RATING: Medium; the stained glass patchwork stitching isn't difficult, but there are lots of pockets to go round!

STITCHING TIP: *Use the continuous piecing method to stitch the strips of binding along the tops of the pockets; hold them under the machine foot one after another, without cutting the sewing threads.*

You will need

- ❋ 36 x 31in (92 x 78cm) printed green fabric for the background
- ❋ 36 x 31in (92 x 78cm) plain green fabric for the backing
- ❋ twenty-four 3½in (9cm) squares of different Christmas print fabrics
- ❋ 12in (30cm) square mottled brown 'gingerbread' fabric
- ❋ 12in (30cm) square white fabric for the icing
- ❋ 5in (13cm) squares of royal blue, yellow and plain green fabrics
- ❋ scraps of light blue fabric for the window and red for the hearts
- ❋ 15yd (15m) black bias binding, ¼in (6mm) wide
- ❋ black and green sewing threads
- ❋ soft pencil
- ❋ extra fabric for a hanging sleeve, or ribbon or tape for display loops
- ❋ assorted round beads in bright colours and different sizes, plus matching threads
- ❋ tube of gold glitter glue or glittery fabric paint

Instructions

Trace or photocopy the gingerbread house design on pages 104-105. Cut the drawing up to make templates, and use these to cut patches from the appropriate fabrics, laying the templates right side up on the right sides of the fabric.

Lay the green print fabric on a flat surface, right side up, and position the patches to assemble the house design in the centre of the panel (**a**). Follow the stitching sequence shown below (**b**) to add the lines of bias binding in order.

a

b

3 Stitch a line of bias binding along the top of each square pocket patch. Then lay the pockets out around the house design; once you're happy with the arrangement, pin them in place (**c**). Stitch a line of bias binding round the remaining three sides of each pocket to secure them to the background (**d**); fold the raw ends under neatly at the tops of the lines.

c

d

4 Using the glitter glue or glittery fabric paint, draw the numbers 1-24 under the pockets, scattering the numbers at random across the design.

5 Put the rectangle of backing fabric and the patchwork design right sides together and stitch a ½in (1cm) seam all the way round; leave an opening of about 12in (30cm) along the bottom edge for turning. Trim the seams, clip the corners and turn the design right side out; press the seams. Turn under the raw edges of the opening and slipstitch it closed.

6 Thread your machine with green thread, and stitch an outline of straight stitch about ½in (1cm) outside the gingerbread house shape.

7 Stitch the beads at random intervals across the icing on the roof, and add a bead in the centre of each diamond shape. Add a hanging sleeve on the back of the panel, or display loops of tape or ribbon at equal intervals along the top edge.

❄ CHRISTMAS IS COMING ❄

Lap Quilt

*A fabulous full-size block quilt in seasonal colours,
stitched in a fraction of the time it takes to do traditional
patchwork! Take all the fiddly bits out of stitching blocks
by assembling them in stained glass patchwork, then quilt
them with big-stitch quilting in coton à broder.*

FINISHED SIZE: just over 5ft (155cm) square

EASINESS RATING: An ambitious project; the stained glass
patchwork side of things is very easy, but there are lots of blocks
and therefore a lot of stitching. Create the whole quilt in easy
stages, or try an individual block as a cushion cover for a very
straightforward project.

STITCHING TIP: *Use rotary cutting to speed up creating the strips and
squares of fabric, and to keep them accurate.*

You will need

❄ 65in (160cm) square of compressed wadding
❄ 65in (160cm) square of red or other backing fabric
❄ 1yd (1m) plain green fabric for the sashing strips
❄ large scraps or various fat quarters of assorted Christmas prints and
plains; you will need about 4sq yd (4sq m) in total
❄ sixteen 12in (30cm) squares of white foundation fabric,
eg lawn or fine calico
❄ coton à broder, two skeins of red and two skeins of green
❄ roughly 55yd (55m) black bias binding, ½in (12mm) wide

❄ 8yd (8m) black bias binding, seam tape or black fabric strips,
2in (5cm) wide, for binding the edges of the quilt
❄ black sewing thread

Instructions

1 From assorted scraps of red print fabric, cut twenty-five
2½in (6cm) squares. From the plain green fabric, cut forty
12 x 2½in (30 x 6cm) strips.

2 There are five different blocks in this quilt: rail fence (**a**),
shoo fly (**b**), pinwheel (**c**), grandmother's fan (**d**), and
crazy (**e**). I've used eight fan blocks (with different
arrangements of fabric), and two blocks of each of the
other four designs, but you can vary them as much as you
like. Each block is made up in the same way. Trace or
photocopy the relevant templates from pages 99-103;
use the templates to cut your fabric patches, then pin the
patches in position on a square of foundation fabric. For
the fan blocks, you will also need a 12in (30cm) square of
Christmas print fabric to make the background of each
block; you can cut away the excess fabric behind the fan
shape if you wish once the patches are in position.

3 Follow the relevant sequence of diagrams (overleaf) to
add the lines of bias binding in order.

4 You now have sixteen stained glass patchwork blocks, and
it's time to assemble them into a quilt top. On a large flat
surface, lay out the sashing strips, the corner squares and the
patchwork blocks as shown (**f**) to create the whole design.

5 Working strip by strip, pin lines of bias binding along
the joins between the patches and stitch in place to
assemble the quilt top (**g**).

6 Lay the large square of backing fabric out
on a flat surface, right side down, and cover
it with the wadding; put the patchwork
design on top, right side up. Secure the
layers using your favourite method –
tacking, safety pins, quilt glue, tack gun etc.
Using the red and green coton à broder,
work big-stitch quilting (just long running
stitches!) ¼in (6mm) inside each patch,
varying the colours as you wish.

7 Bind the edges of the quilt with the
wider binding or tape, or the strips of
black fabric.

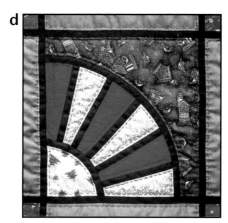

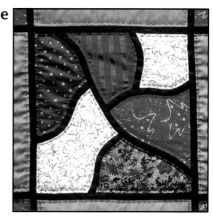

THE PROJECTS: CHRISTMAS IS COMING **55**

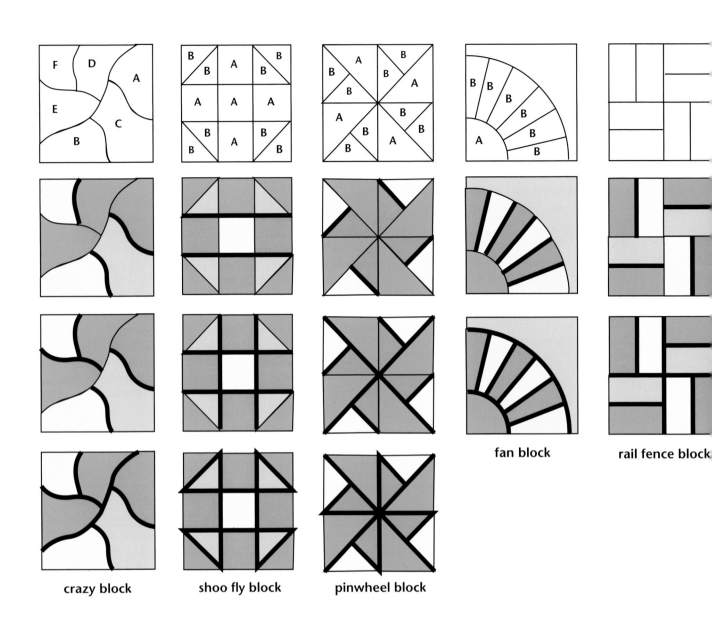

crazy block

shoo fly block

pinwheel block

fan block

rail fence block

f

fan	pinwheel	fan	rail fence
shoo fly	fan	crazy	fan
fan	rail fence	fan	pinwheel
crazy	fan	shoo fly	fan

g

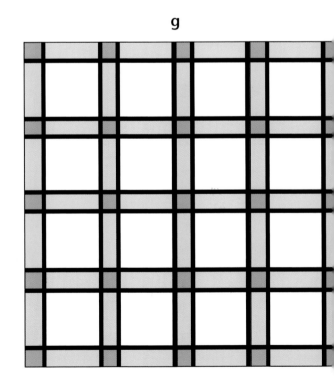

THE PROJECTS: CHRISTMAS IS COMING

The Templates

THE TEMPLATES

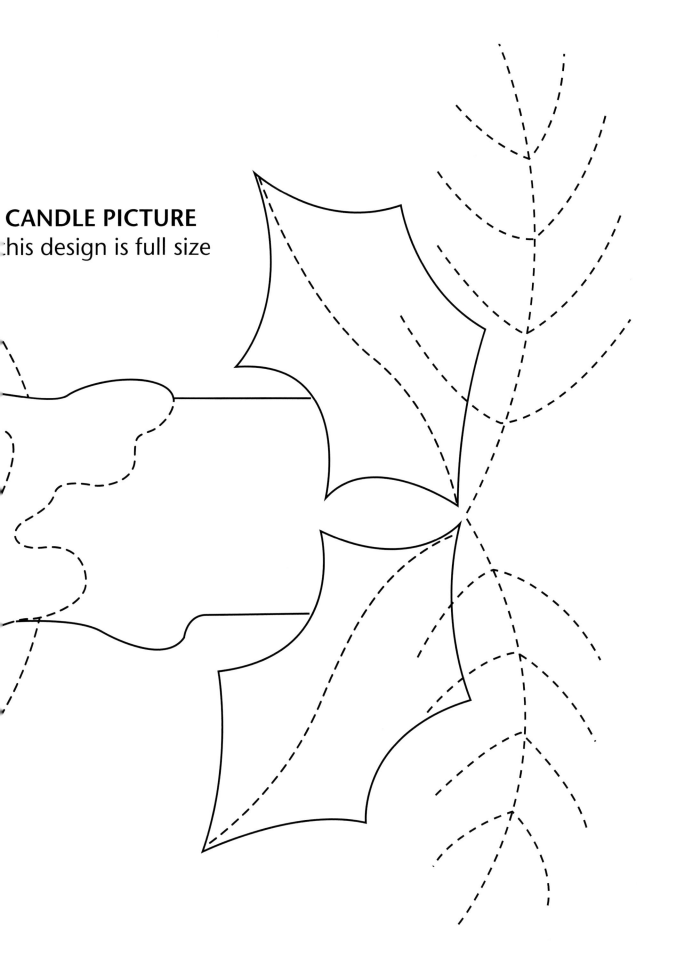

CANDLE PICTURE
this design is full size

CHRISTMAS GREENERY
table runner
this design is full size

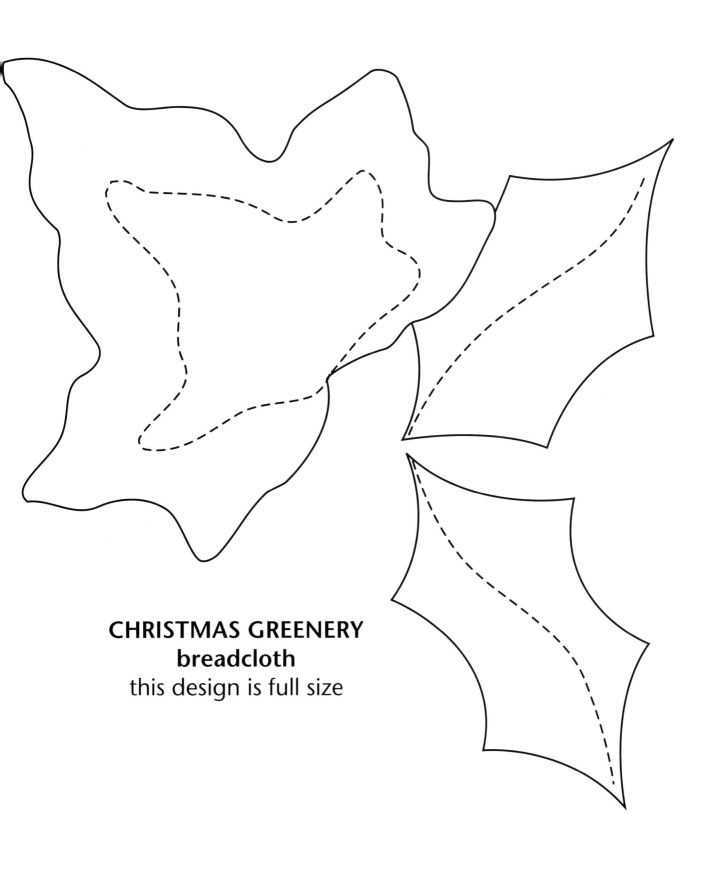

CHRISTMAS GREENERY
breadcloth
this design is full size

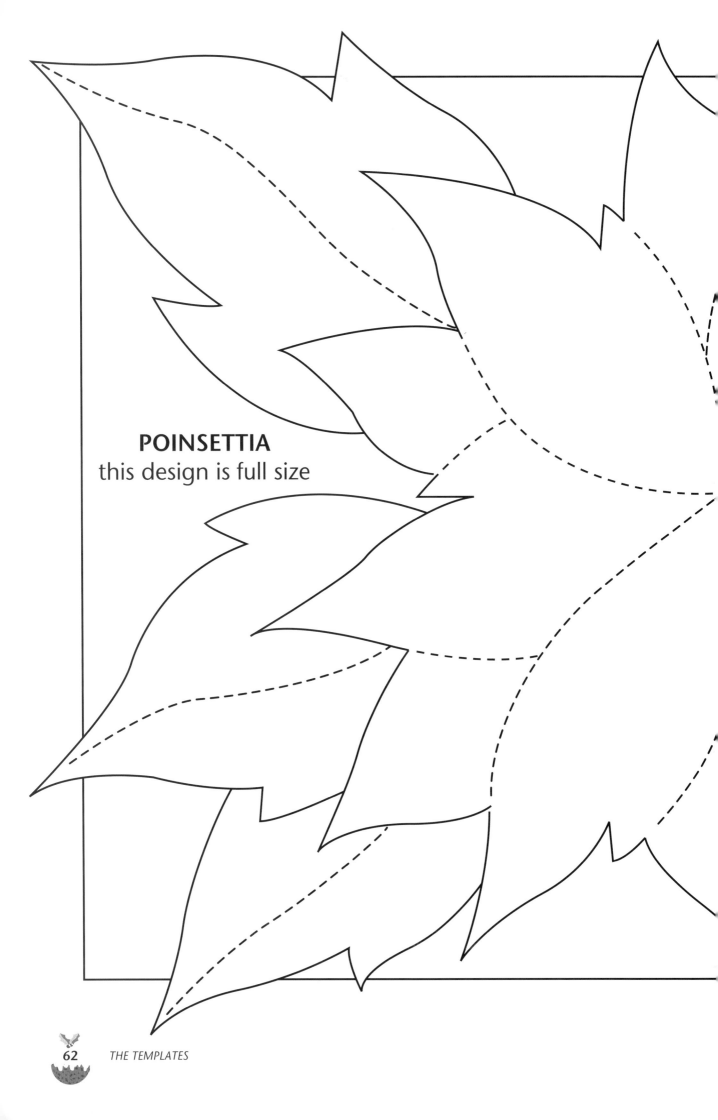

POINSETTIA
this design is full size

PARTRIDGE IN A PEAR TREE
this design is full size

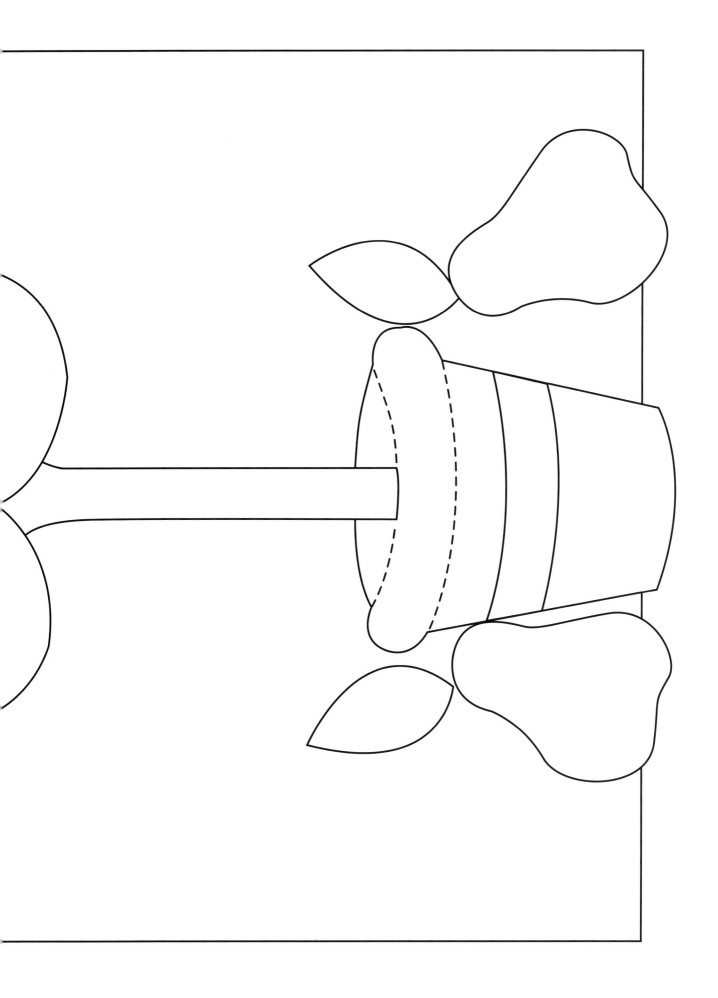

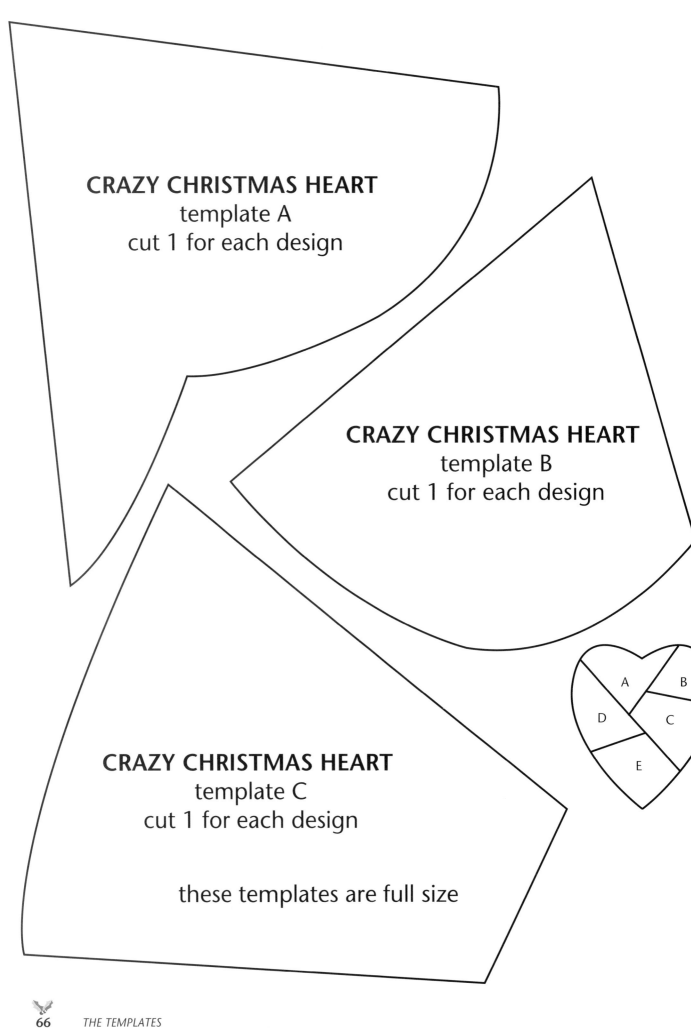

CRAZY CHRISTMAS HEART
template A
cut 1 for each design

CRAZY CHRISTMAS HEART
template B
cut 1 for each design

CRAZY CHRISTMAS HEART
template C
cut 1 for each design

these templates are full size

these templates are full size

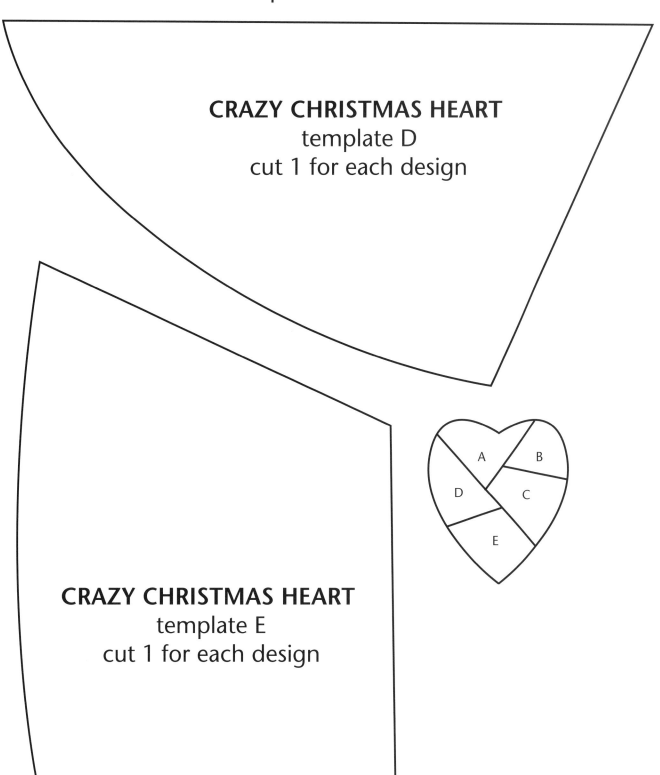

CRAZY CHRISTMAS HEART
template D
cut 1 for each design

CRAZY CHRISTMAS HEART
template E
cut 1 for each design

A

B

D

C

E

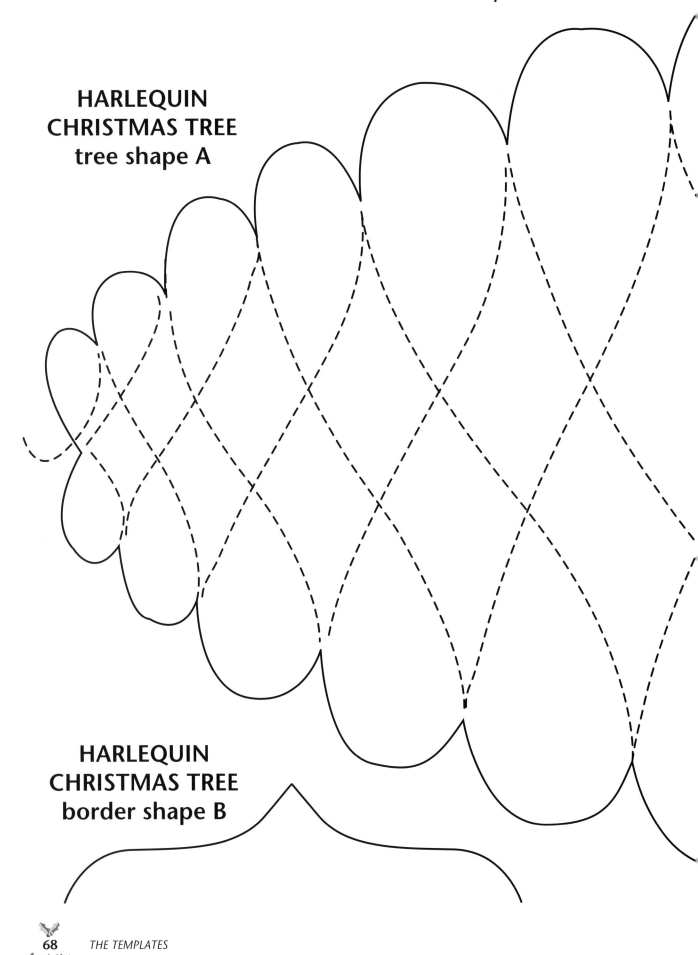

**HARLEQUIN
CHRISTMAS TREE
tree shape A**

**HARLEQUIN
CHRISTMAS TREE
border shape B**

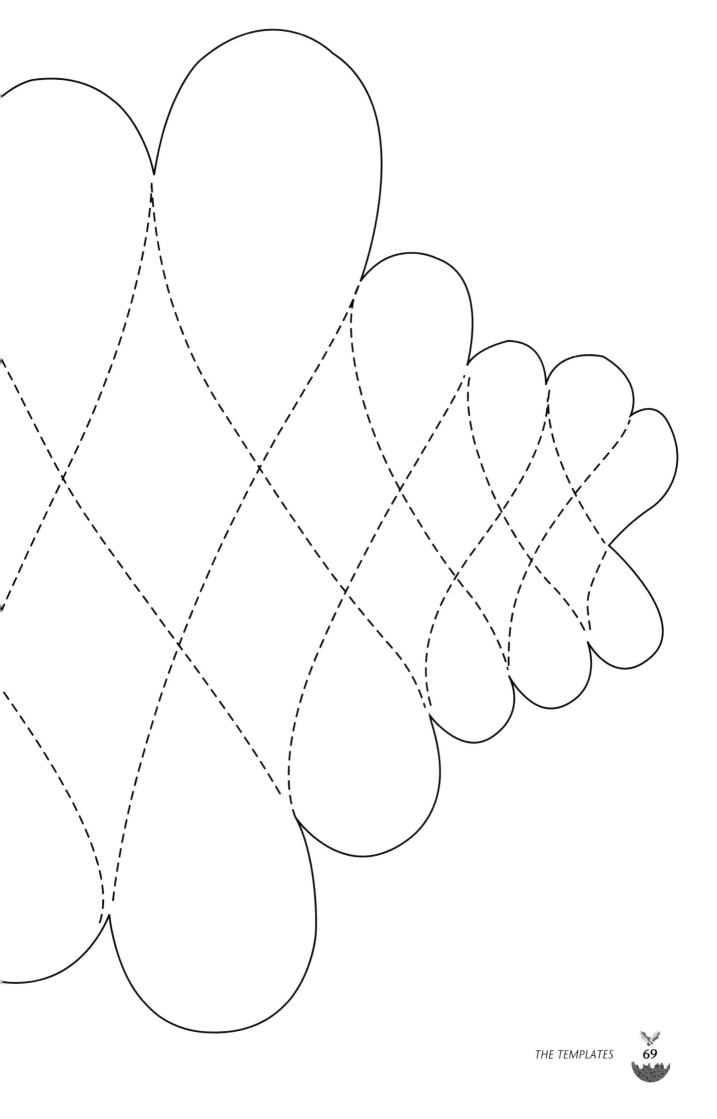

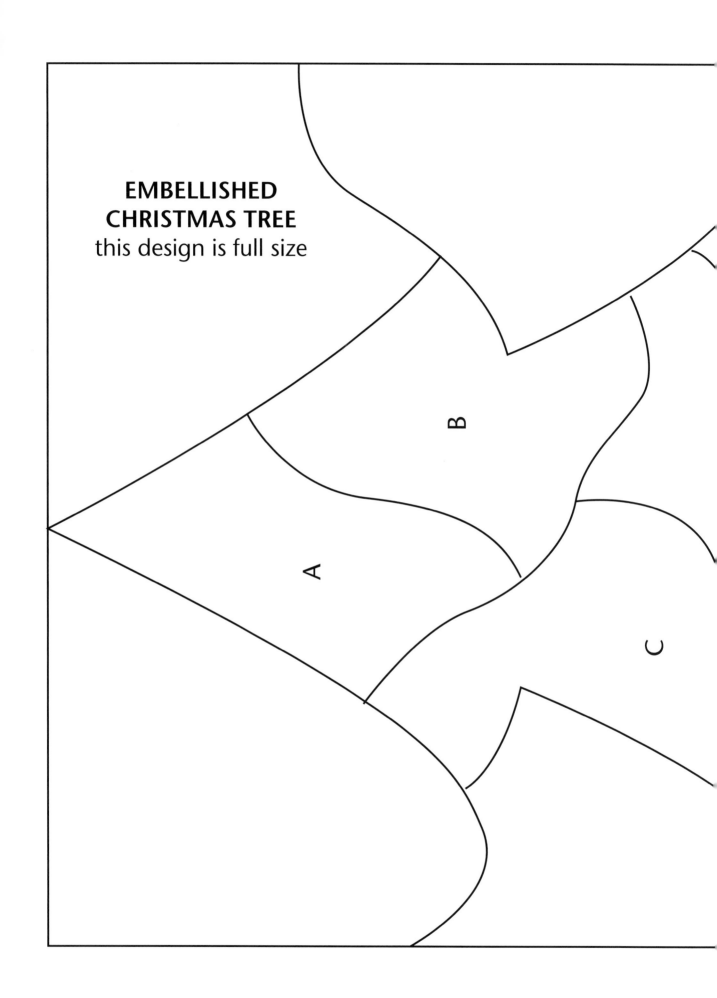

EMBELLISHED CHRISTMAS TREE
this design is full size

A

B

C

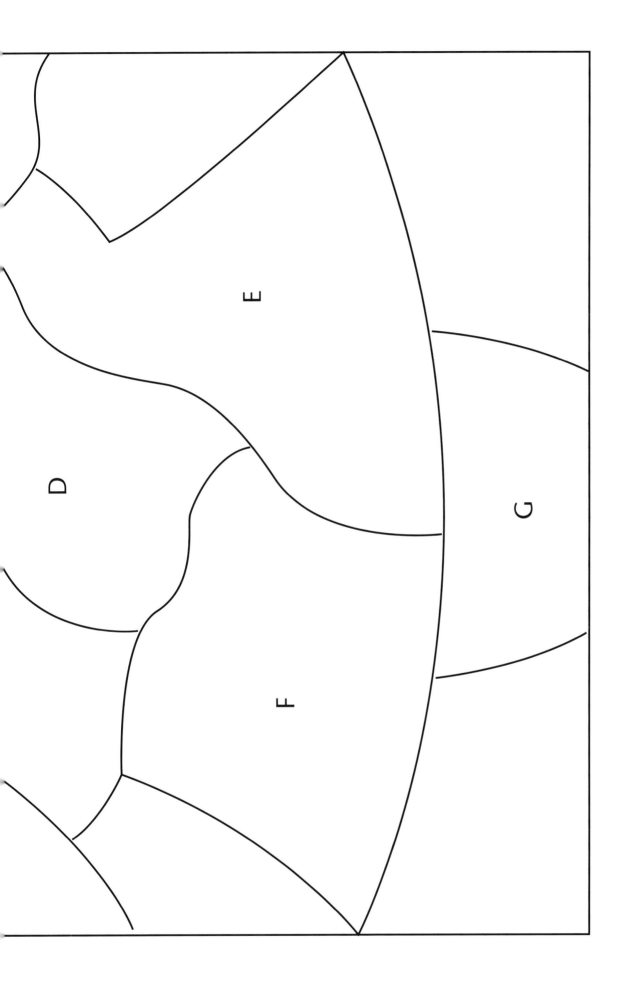

DOVE
each square of the grid = 10in (25cm)

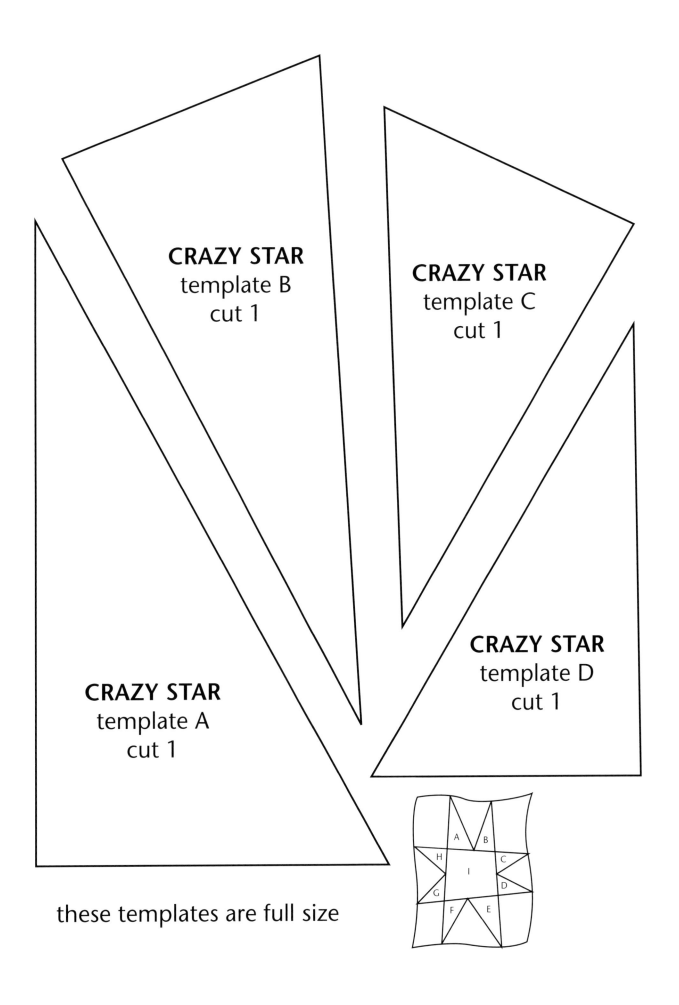

CRAZY STAR
template B
cut 1

CRAZY STAR
template C
cut 1

CRAZY STAR
template A
cut 1

CRAZY STAR
template D
cut 1

these templates are full size

these templates are full size

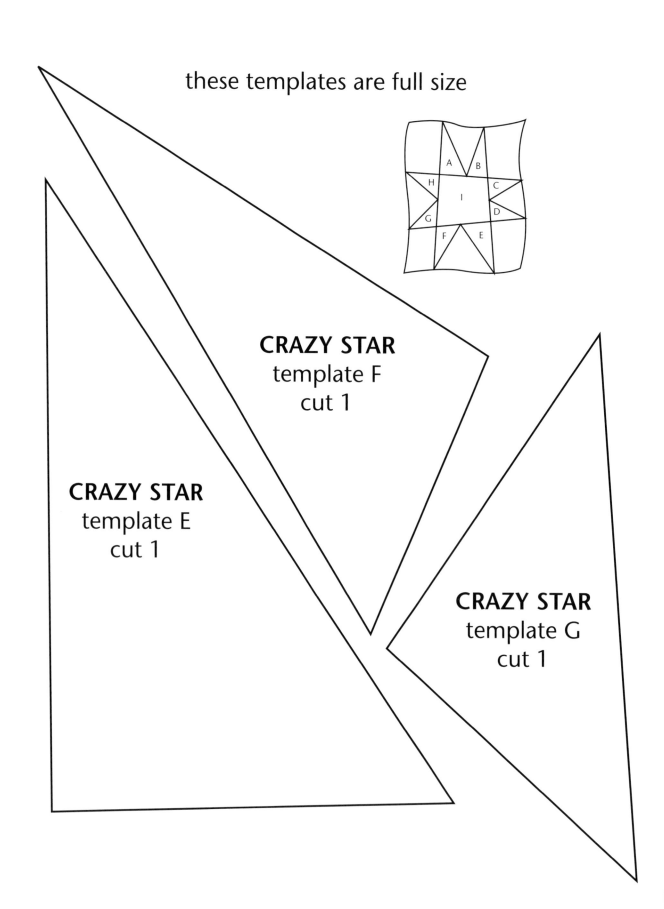

CRAZY STAR
template F
cut 1

CRAZY STAR
template E
cut 1

CRAZY STAR
template G
cut 1

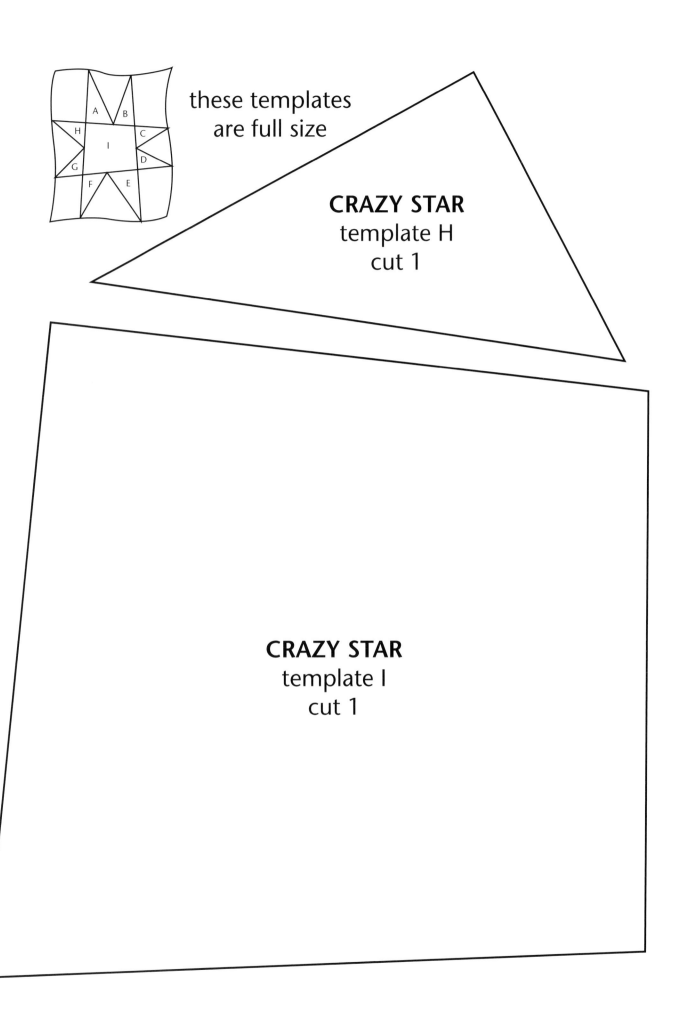

these templates
are full size

CRAZY STAR
template H
cut 1

CRAZY STAR
template I
cut 1

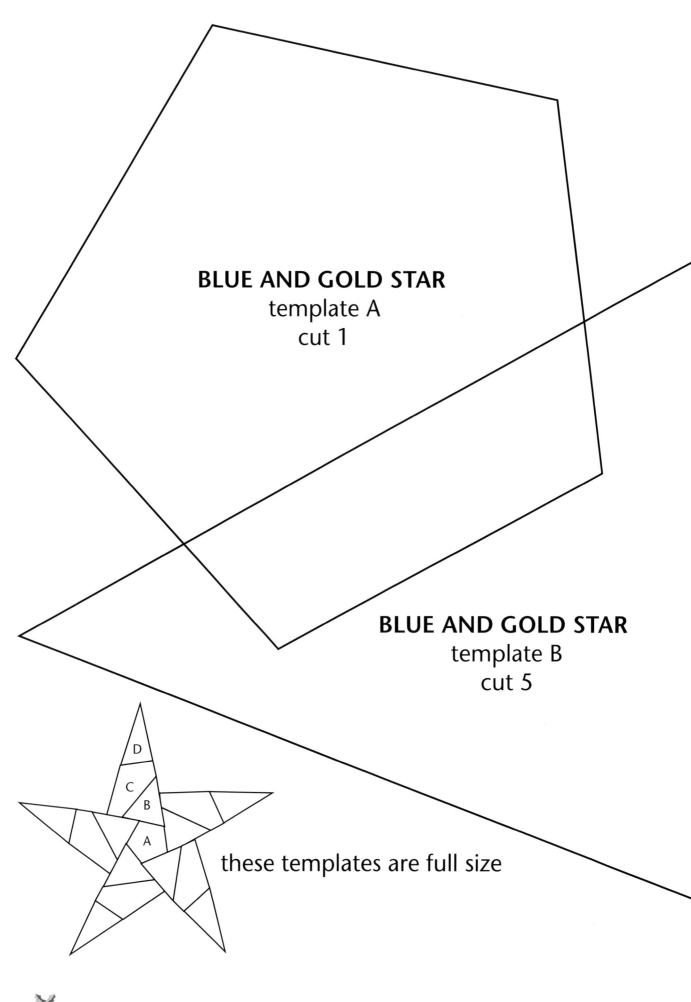

BLUE AND GOLD STAR
template A
cut 1

BLUE AND GOLD STAR
template B
cut 5

these templates are full size

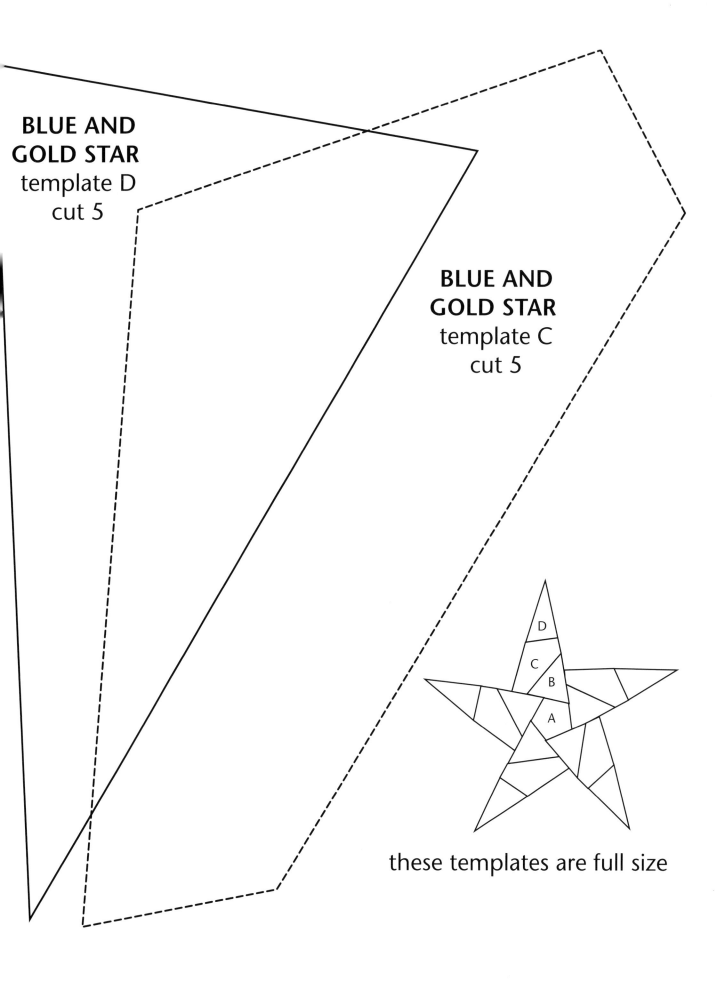

BLUE AND GOLD STAR
template D
cut 5

BLUE AND GOLD STAR
template C
cut 5

these templates are full size

CHURCH WINDOW
window shape A
this design is full size,
and forms half of the
window top

centre line

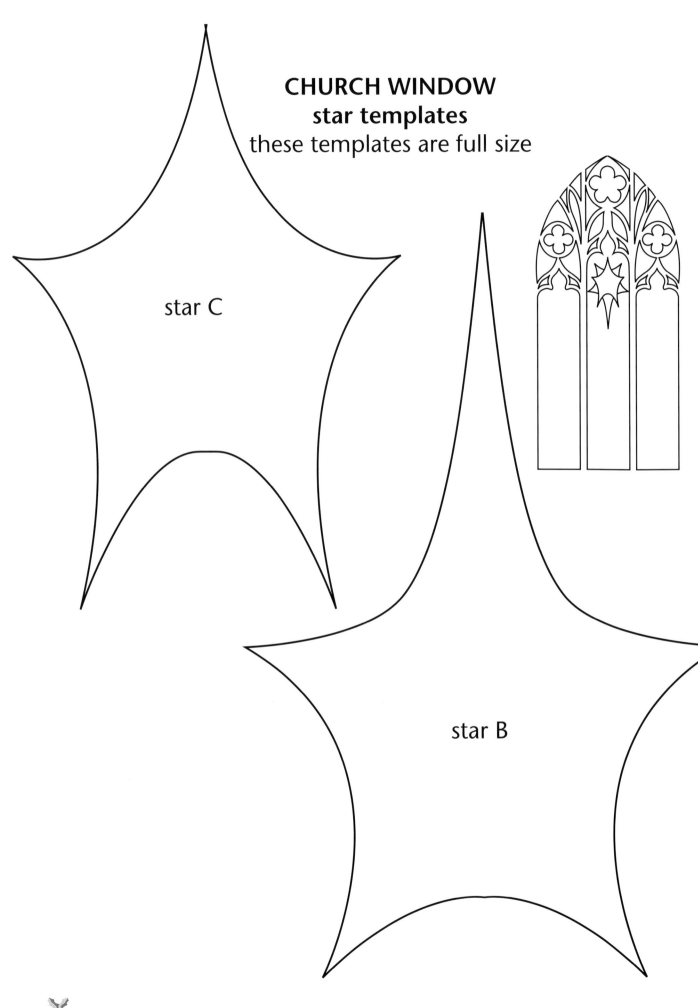

CHURCH WINDOW
star templates
these templates are full size

star C

star B

ANGEL
each square of the grid = 4in (10cm)

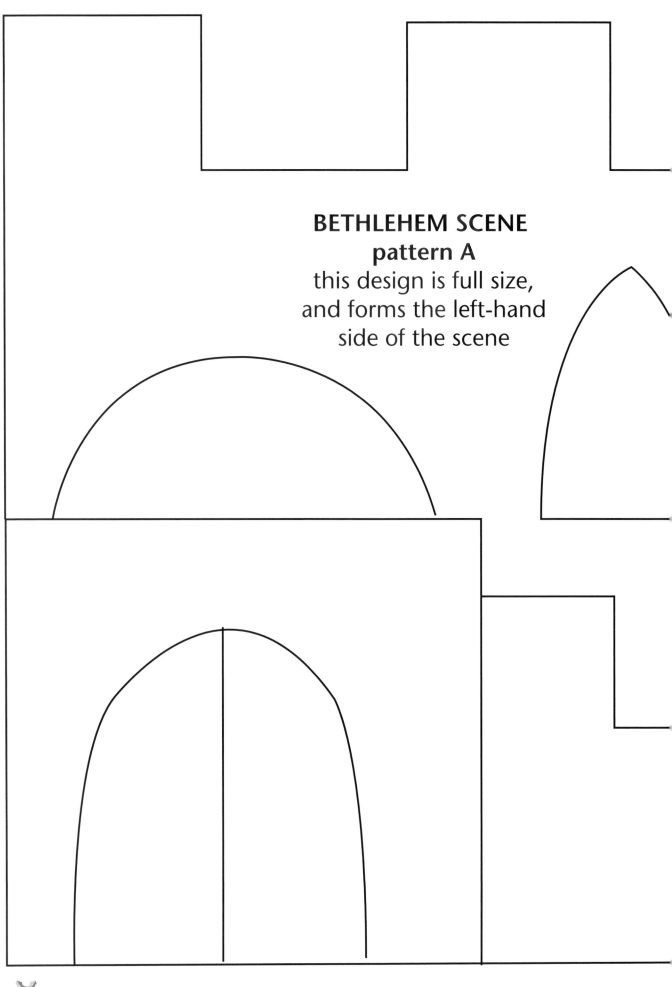

BETHLEHEM SCENE
pattern A
this design is full size,
and forms the left-hand
side of the scene

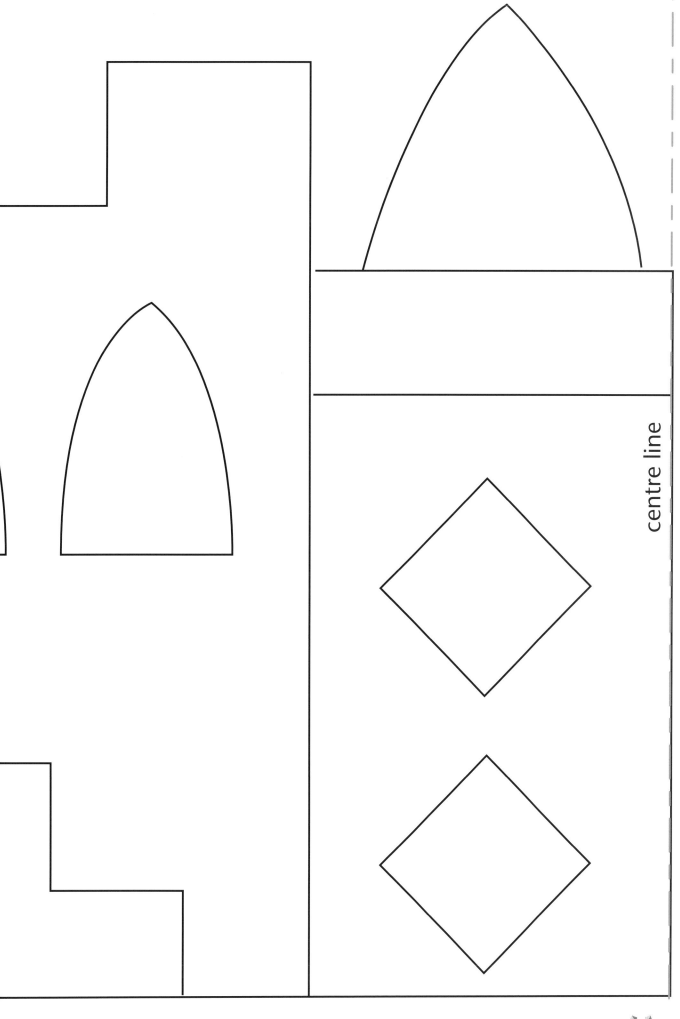

centre line

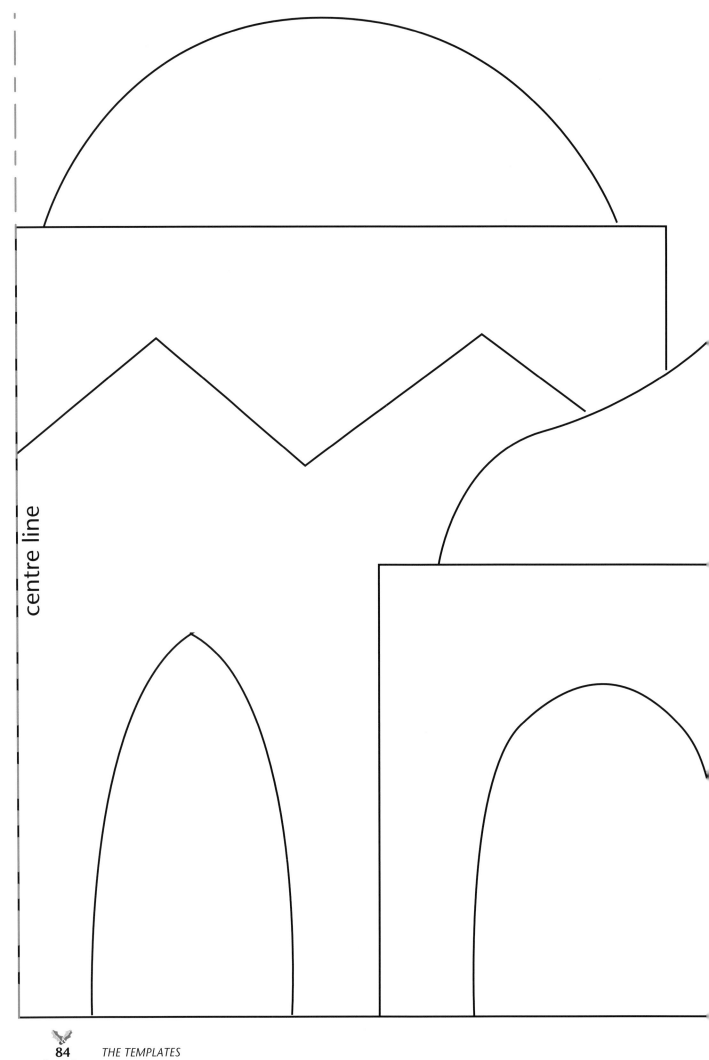

centre line

BETHLEHEM SCENE
pattern B
this design is full size,
and forms the right-hand
side of the scene

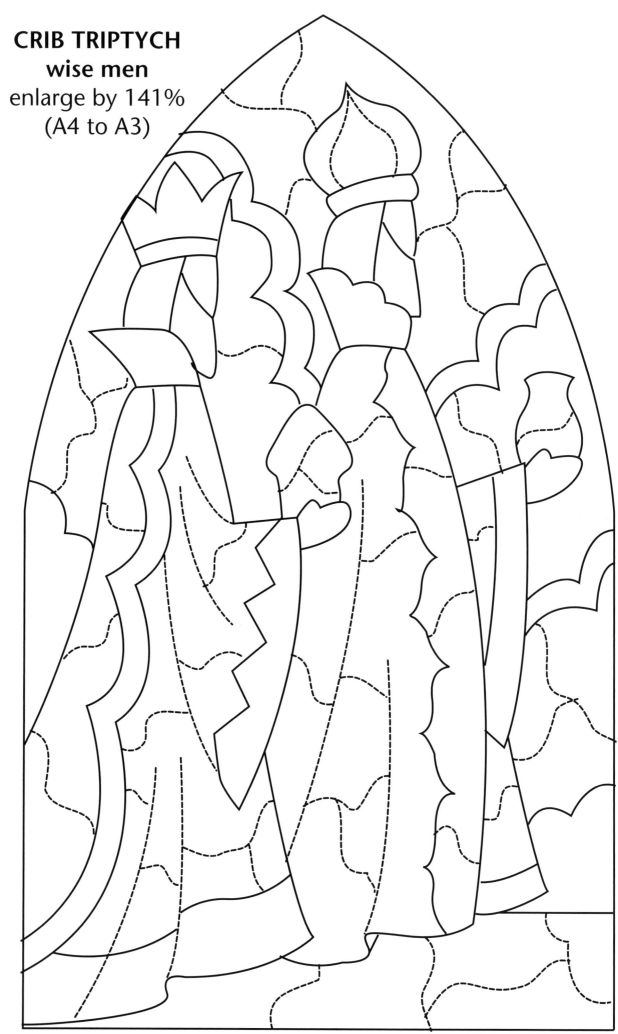

CRIB TRIPTYCH
wise men
enlarge by 141%
(A4 to A3)

CRIB TRIPTYCH
holy family
enlarge by 141%
(A4 to A3)

CRIB TRIPTYCH
shepherds
enlarge by 141%
(A4 to A3)

SNOW-SCENE STOCKING
this design is full size

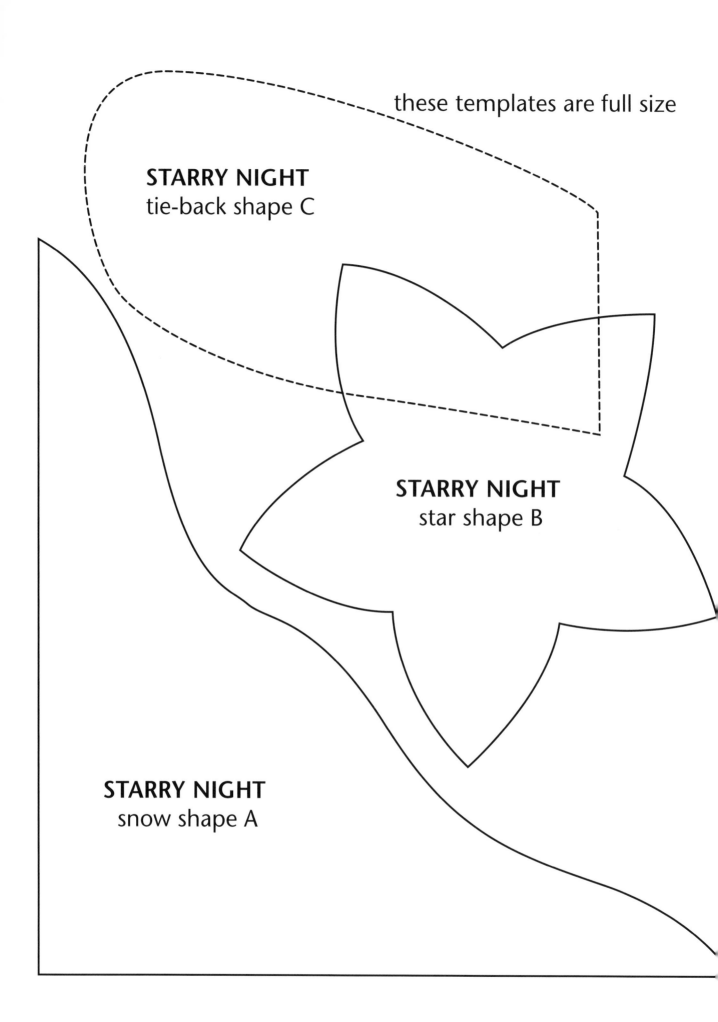

these templates are full size

STARRY NIGHT
tie-back shape C

STARRY NIGHT
star shape B

STARRY NIGHT
snow shape A

MIDNIGHT SKIES
pattern A for casement window

this design is full size

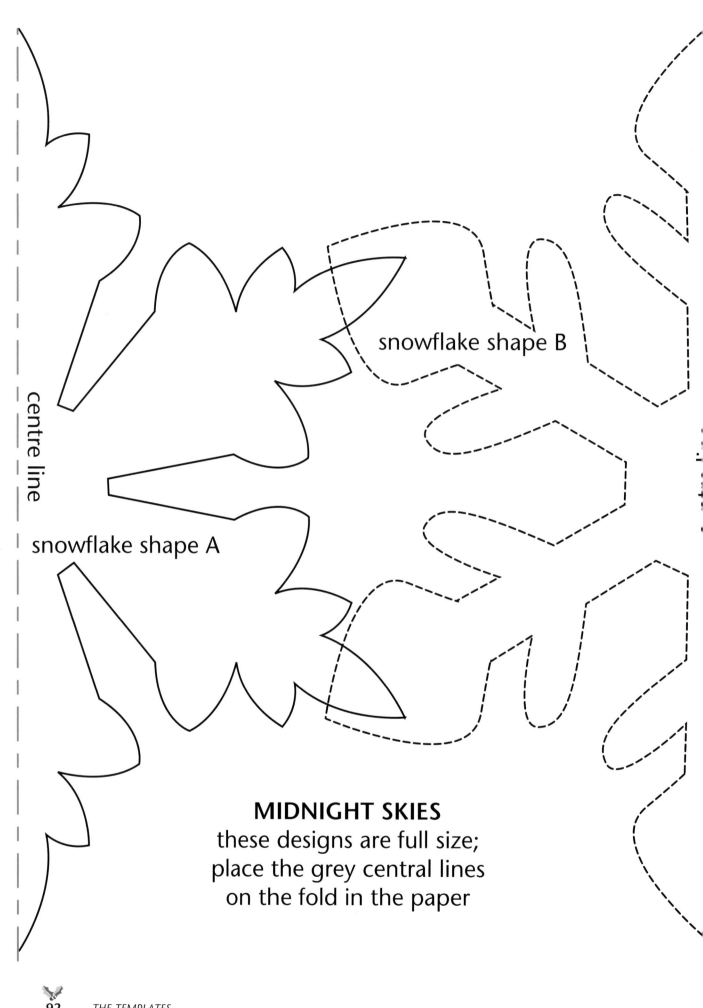

centre line

snowflake shape A

snowflake shape B

MIDNIGHT SKIES
these designs are full size;
place the grey central lines
on the fold in the paper

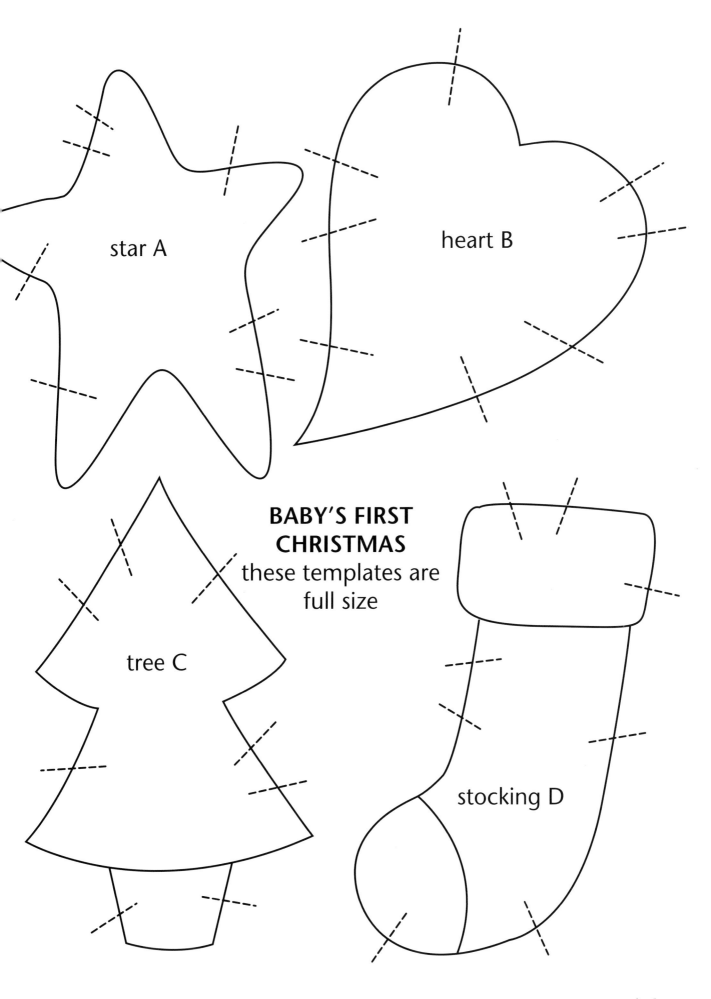

star A

heart B

**BABY'S FIRST
CHRISTMAS**
these templates are
full size

tree C

stocking D

CHRISTMAS KEEPSAKE ALBUM
this design is full size

NOEL
template for N

this design is full size

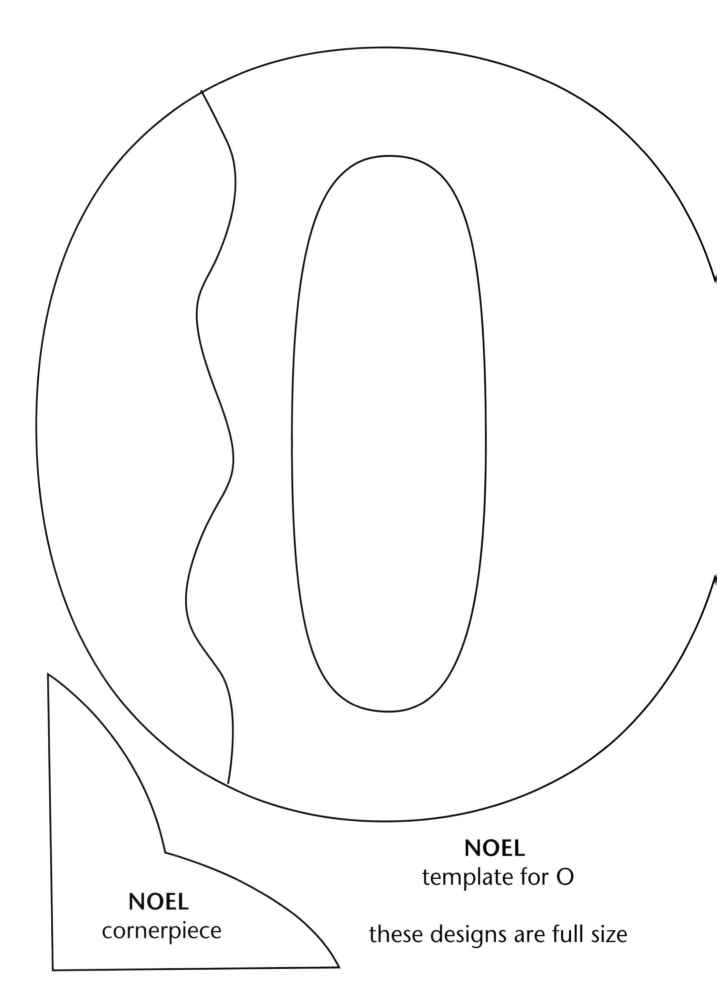

NOEL
template for O

these designs are full size

NOEL
cornerpiece

NOEL
template for E

this design is full size

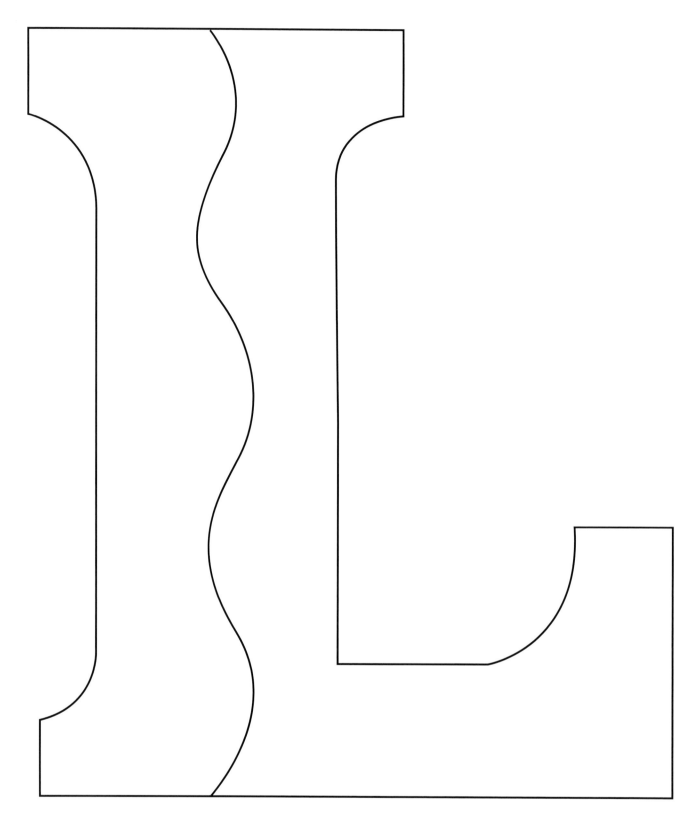

NOEL
template for L

this design is full size

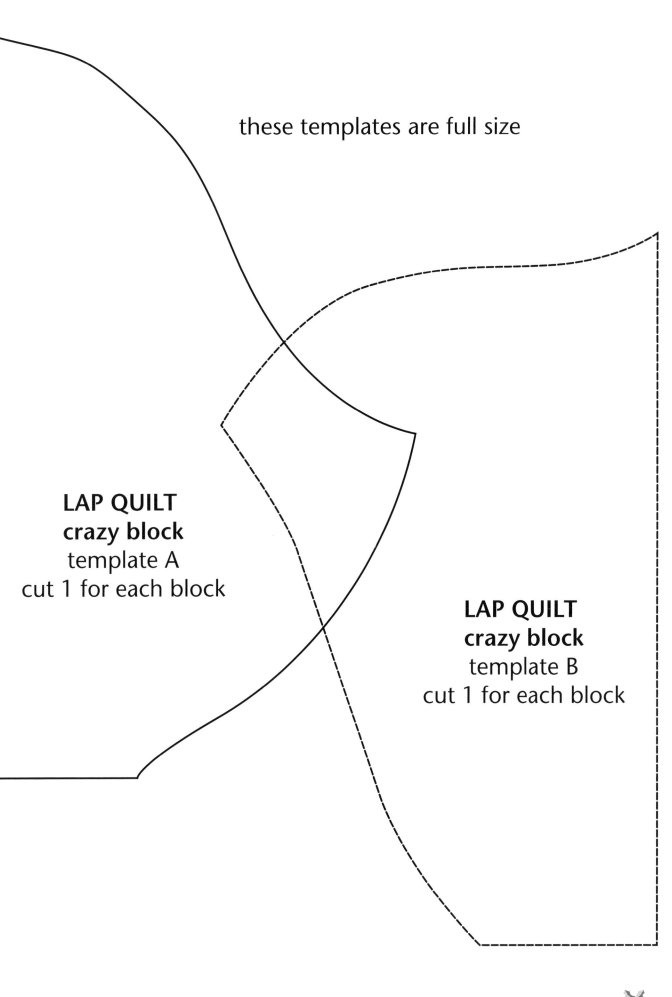

these templates are full size

**LAP QUILT
crazy block
template A
cut 1 for each block**

**LAP QUILT
crazy block
template B
cut 1 for each block**

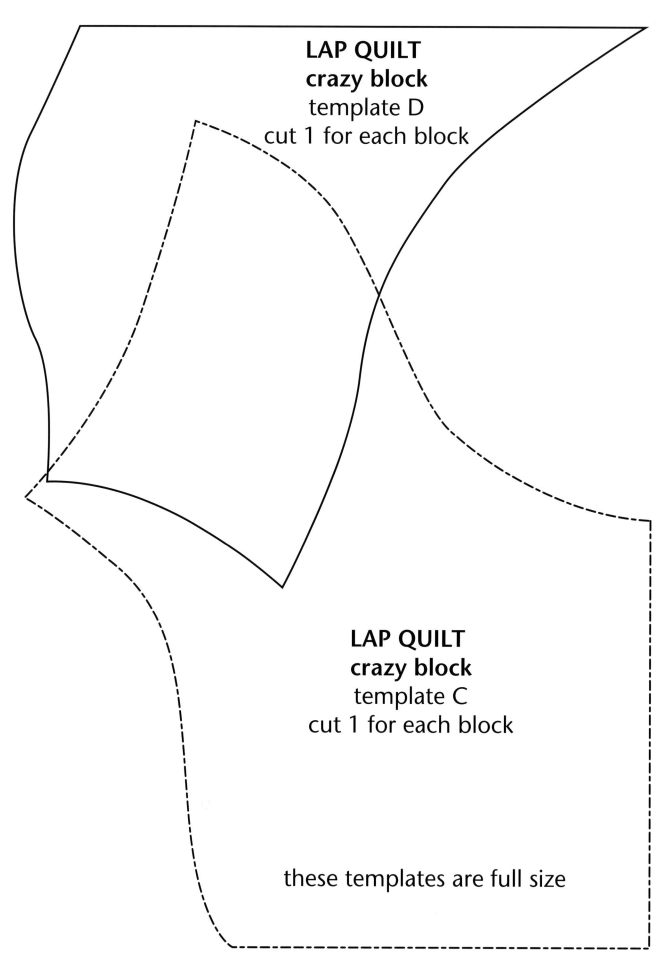

LAP QUILT
crazy block
template D
cut 1 for each block

LAP QUILT
crazy block
template C
cut 1 for each block

these templates are full size

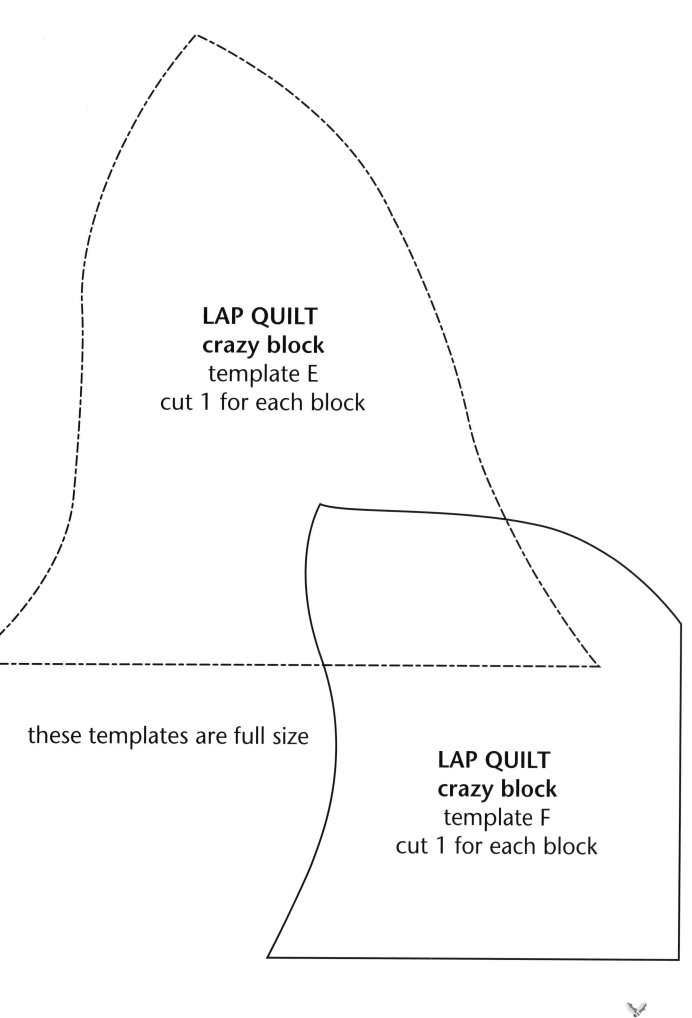

LAP QUILT
crazy block
template E
cut 1 for each block

these templates are full size

LAP QUILT
crazy block
template F
cut 1 for each block

**LAP QUILT
fan block
template A
cut 1 for each block**

these templates are full size

**LAP QUILT
fan block
template B
cut a total of 6
for each block**

**LAP QUILT
rail fence block
template
cut a total of 8
for each block**

these templates are full size

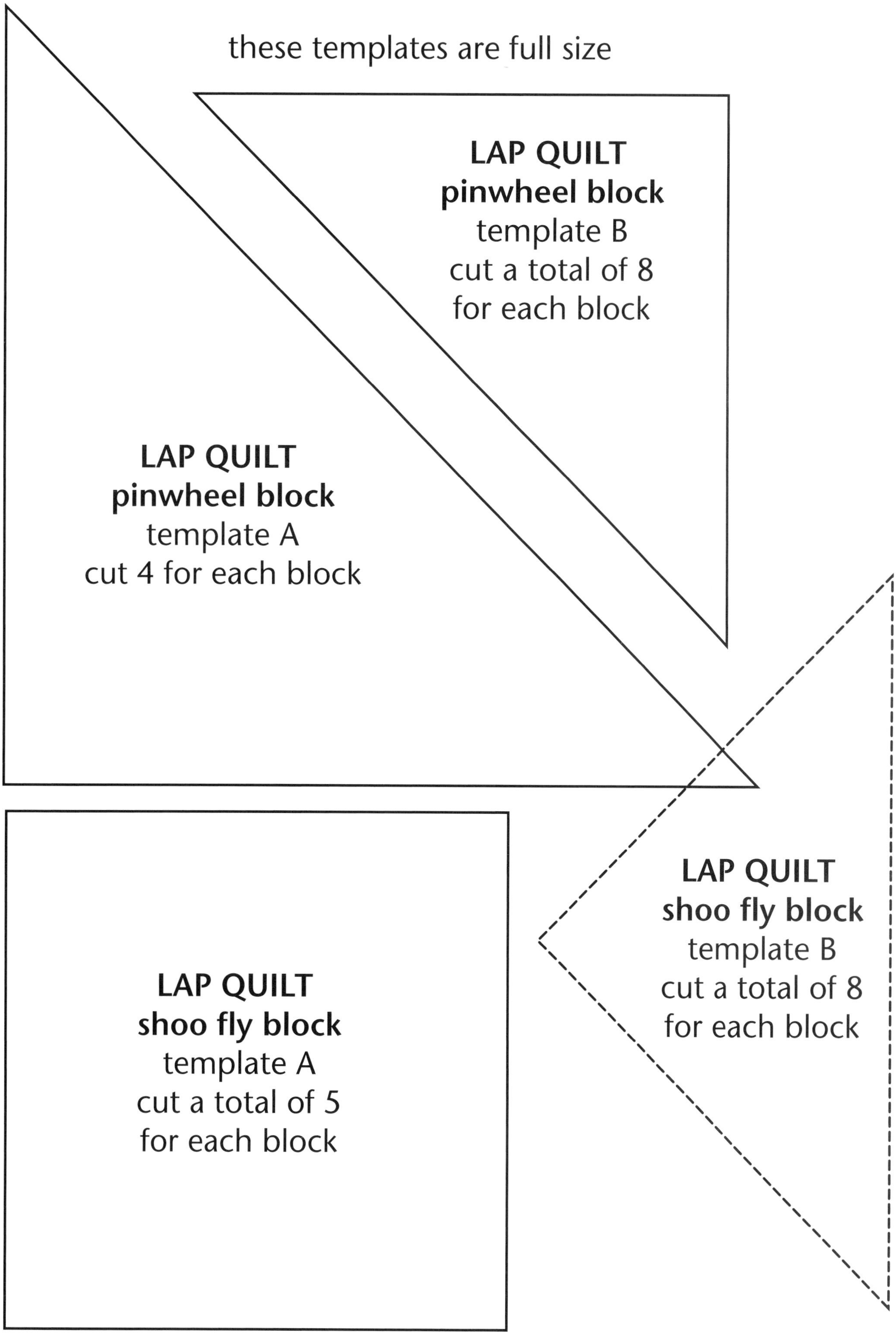

LAP QUILT
pinwheel block
template B
cut a total of 8
for each block

LAP QUILT
pinwheel block
template A
cut 4 for each block

LAP QUILT
shoo fly block
template A
cut a total of 5
for each block

LAP QUILT
shoo fly block
template B
cut a total of 8
for each block

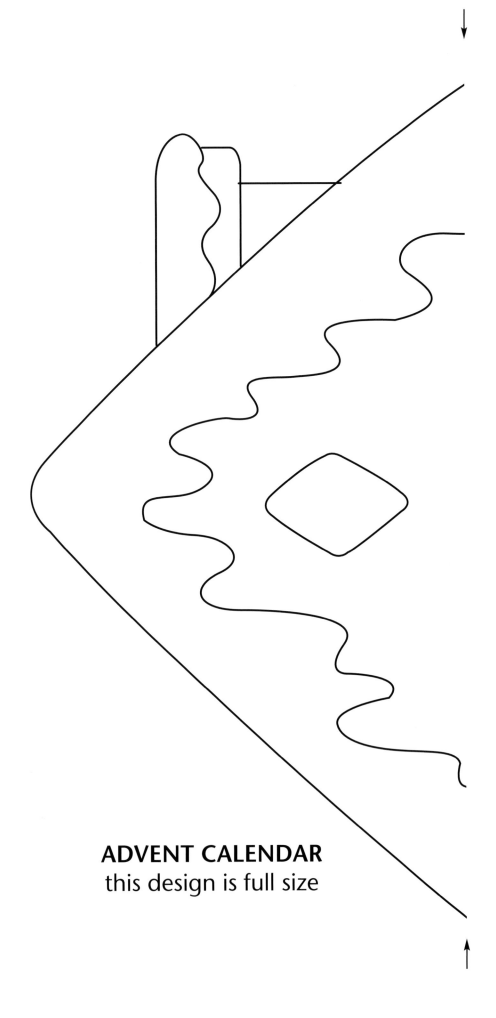

ADVENT CALENDAR
this design is full size

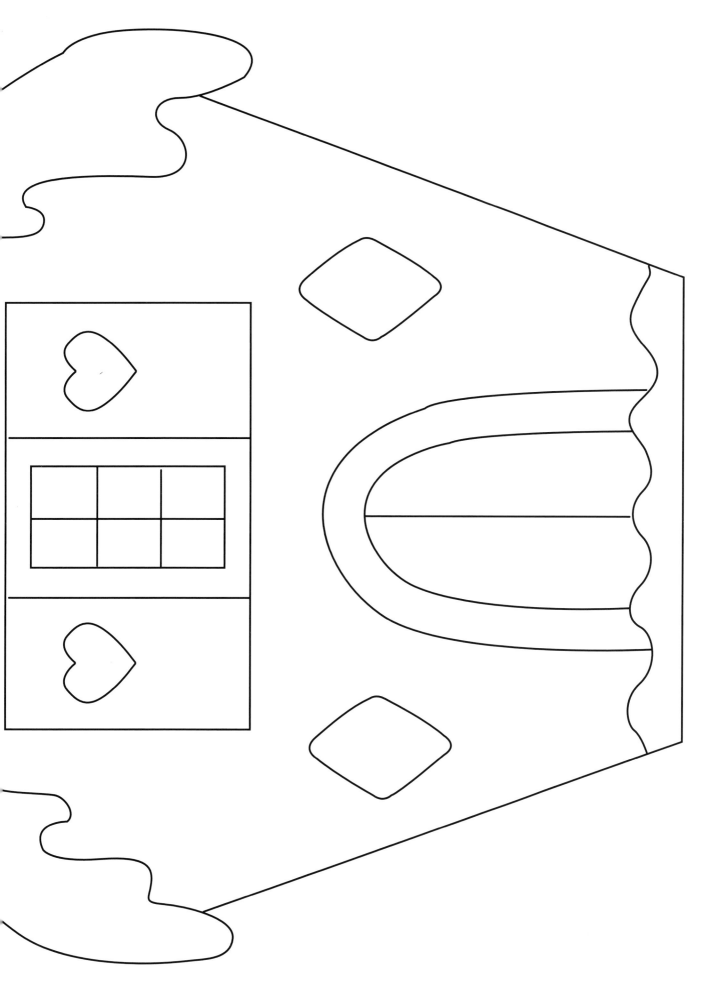

**TURTLE DOVES
the 2nd day
of Christmas**
enlarge this design
by 141% (A4 to A3)

FRENCH HENS
the 3rd day of Christmas
enlarge this design by 141%
(A4 to A3)

CALLING BIRDS
the 4th day of Christmas
enlarge this design by
141% (A4 to A3)

GOLD RINGS
the 5th day of Christmas
enlarge this design by 141%
(A4 to A3)

LAYING GOOSE
the 6th day of Christmas
enlarge this design by 141%
(A4 to A3)

SWIMMING SWAN
the 7th day of Christmas
enlarge this design by 141%
(A4 to A3)

MAID MILKING
the 8th day of Christmas
enlarge this design by
141% (A4 to A3)

DRUMMER
the 9th day of Christmas
enlarge this design by 141%
(A4 to A3)

PIPER
the 10th day of Christmas
enlarge this design by 141%
(A4 to A3)